CW01347733

Biography of NIGERIA'S FOREMOST PROFESSOR OF STATISTICS PROF. JAMES NWOYE ADICHIE

By

Emeritus Prof. Alex Animalu

Prof. Peter I. Uche

Jeff Unaegbu

BIOGRAPHY OF NIGERIA'S FOREMOST PROFESSOR OF STATISTICS JAMES NWOYE ADICHIE

By
ALEX ANIMALU
PETER I. UCHE
JEFF UNAEGBU

Copyright © 2013 by Alex Animalu, Peter Uche & Jeff Unaegbu

All Rights Reserved
This book or any part thereof must not be reproduced in any form without the written permission of the Copyright Owners.

National Library of Nigeria Cataloguing in Publication Data

1. **Title: Biography of Nigeria's Foremost Professor of Statistics, James Nwoye Adichie**
2. **Authors: Alex Animalu, Peter Uche & Jeff Unaegbu**

ISBN: 9798592635113
Published by: Ucheakonam Foundation @ International Centre for Basic Research, 20 Limpopo St. FHA, Maitama, Abuja, Nigeria.
Phone: +234 803 787 9351

Printed in Nigeria by:
University of Nigeria Press Ltd.
Bookshop/ Bank Complex, University of Nigeria, Nsukka
Phone: +234 (0)7038627778

FOREWORD

Writing a foreword to the biography of a phenomenon as large as Prof. J.N. Adichie (James) is certainly an intriguing experience. Fortunately, my knowledge of him makes the task less daunting than it would otherwise have been. James achieved greatness by dint of hard work. His rise to stardom started when his caring father, a disciplinarian, carried him regularly on his bicycle from Abba through the winding roads then to Nimo some kilometers away where he was able to pursue his primary school education. I believe that this experience inspired the young James and made a lasting impression on him as amply illustrated in *Biography of Nigeria's Foremost Professor of Statistics, James Nwoye Adichie.*

I have had the privilege of being a very close classmate of James during our days at the Mathematics Department in the University College, Ibadan, between 1957 and 1960. James, Charles Olusegun Sowunmi (now of blessed memory) and I graduated in 1960 as the top three in a class of 13. The late renowned Professor Chike Obi, our teacher and the first Nigerian to obtain a Ph.D. in mathematics used to refer to James and me as brothers because he thought we looked very much alike. James went on to become the first Professor of Statistics in Nigeria in October, 1976 and I later became the second one in May, 1977. It is wonderful that destiny has allowed this story of him to be written. The story of my own life is told in my book, *In His Hands: The Autobiography of a Nigerian Village Boy,* published in 2005. It is refreshing and remarkable to note that, come this December 2013, the story of the life of Segun will be told in the forthcoming book, *OLUSEGUN SOWUNMI: An Extraordinary and Quiet Achiever,* by M. Adebisi Sowunmi, his beloved widow, and a retired Professor of Archeology. This will complete the narrations of the life histories of the three 'stars'. I am happy that there are also biographies on the mathematical geniuses and university administrators as the late Professor J.O.C. Ezeilo and Professor (Senator) Iya Abubakar, the only two students to have made first class honours in Mathematics as at the time that we graduated in 1960.

The enormous achievements in the many theatres of James' life are well chronicled in this biography. It is documentation for posterity and one which celebrates a life of accomplishments, courage and determination as exemplified by, among others, his harrowing experiences during the rather unfortunate Nigeria-Biafra civil war, 1967-1970. James has had a tremendous salutary influence on the Nigerian statistics terrain. From the moment providence chose a career for him as a statistician, he has been all sorts of positive and defining things to the statistics world. He has been a distinguished teacher, a role model and a mentor to generations of successful Nigerians. He was a regular author and a reviewer of many articles in several reputable Journals of Statistics. He has been very active and visible in shaping the course of statistics in the University system. It is thus proper and fitting that his story be told from the roof tops. In the Nigerian *Guardian* newspaper of May 28, 2009, I had started this crusade in an article titled *James Nwoye Adichie; Nigeria's First Professor of Statistics.* This book is a fitting culmination of that crusade. I feel highly honoured to write the foreword to the biography of an illustrious son of Abba, a quiet and humble achiever and father of statistics in Nigeria. I congratulate the authors for a job well done.

Prof. Biyi Afonja

PREFACE/ ACKNOWLEDGEMENTS

Writing a biography of the first Professor of Statistics in Nigeria is historical in that the world needs to know how and why Statistics became a serious field of study in Nigeria through the pioneering works of early statisticians. Accompanying this basic reason is the curious fact that the person of James Adichie is quiet and unassuming. And largely, because of this personality factor, his works have been shortchanged by popular history. Another reason for trying to decipher the James Adichie niche is his style of leadership. He has successfully led his children to enviable heights of emulation; one of them is the well-known international author, Chimamanda Ngozi Adichie. Prof. Adichie's wife also caught her husband's fire by becoming the first female Registrar of the University of Nigeria. One of the biographers, Prof. Peter Ikechukwu Uche, a product of Prof. Adichie's statistical prowess became the best graduating student in the University of Nigeria and is today a giant in a class of his own.

Adichie was part of the twelve-man Ad-Hoc Committee set up to establish the National Mathematical Centre in Nigeria by 1987. He was present at the first meeting for the kick-off plan of the Centre. He was the brain behind the statistical ideas inserted into the proposal for the founding of the NMC. He was later appointed a coordinator of the statistics programme of the NMC. Adichie majorly founded the first department of Statistics in eastern Nigeria, served as its Head of Department, then later as Dean of a faculty and then

Deputy Vice Chancellor before moving to NMC. Today, Adichie is still very strong at 81 and drives himself around town! The source of this strength and many other secrets are revealed in his philosophy of life.

This biography may well make a clarion call to the importance of research and memory in the life of a nation. We hope that many biographies of academic pioneers will follow suit and form a large pool of memory which will guide us all to that destiny of a powerful nation which we all dream about.

We acknowledge the support of the Adichie family, especially Prof. James Adichie, *Odeluora n'abba,* for availing us information through interviews and manuscripts despite the constraints on his time and energy. We also say grateful thanks to the Department of Statistics for their support. Our families have been most caring through this period of momentary isolation into piles of dusty files and meditation which every research journey is accustomed to. We say thank you once again.

Des gustibus, non est disputandum.

2306 hours, June 22, 2013
Nsukka

Alex Animalu
Peter Uche
Jeff Unaegbu

TABLE OF CONTENTS

PICTURE GALLERY

1987: Professor James Adichie (c) poses with members of the Students' Statistical Association of the University of Nigeria, Nsukka

1987: Professor James Adichie (c) with Mr. Emeka Okubike (3rd from left) pose with members of the Students' Statistical Association of the UNN

1987: Prof. Adichie and wife, Mrs. Grace Adichie (left and right respectively) pose with their first daughter, Ijeoma (2nd from right) and second daughter, Uche (2nd from left) during their graduation from the University of Nigeria, Nsukka

1987: Prof. Adichie and wife, Mrs. Grace Adichie (2nd from left and1st from right respectively) pose with their children during their graduation from the University of Nigeria, Nsukka

Prof. James Adichie during his graduation from the University College, Ibadan on December 3, 1960

1982: Prof. James Adichie (as Deputy Vice Chancellor, Nsukka campus) standing behind the University Registrar, Mr. Umeh, during a University procession

Prof. James Adichie (centre in gray suit) and some staff members of the Department of Statistics pose with final year students of the Department (class of 1987)

Prof. Adichie during his conferment with the chieftaincy title of *Odeluora* n'Abba by the Igwe of Abba town, HRH L.N. Ezeh (Eze Abba)

Prof. Adichie as knight of St. Mulumba in full regalia of 4th degree (March, 2004)

Prof. James Adichie poses with his PhD academic gown

Self-Portrait: Prof. James Adichie poses with his PhD academic gown

Prof. Adichie delivering an address during an academic function in the University of Nigeria, Nsukka

Prof. Adichie in native attire

Prof. James Adichie as an assistant lecturer in the University of Nigeria in 1961

Prof. Adichie as a young undergraduate student at the University College, Ibadan in 1958

1987: Prof. James Nwoye Adichie as Professor of Statistics

Prof. Adichie poses with his family in 1983. (Back row, L-R: Prof. Adichie, Ijeoma (1st daughter), Chuks (1st son), Uchenna (2nd daughter), Mrs. Grace Adichie (wife); Front row (L-R): Okechukwu (2nd son), Kenechukwu (last son), Ngozi Chimamanda (last daughter)

Erich Leo Lehmann: Adichie's PhD Supervisor at University of California, Berkeley

Jerzy Neyman: Erich Leo Lehmann's Supervisor/ Advisor

A Google Satellite map showing a part of Abba town with actual features

The topographic map of the above satellite capture

L-R: Prof. Animalu, Prof. James Adichie and Jeff Unaegbu

L-R (Authors): Prof. Alex Animalu, Prof. Peter I. Uche and Jeff Unaegbu

FAMILY GENEOLOGY

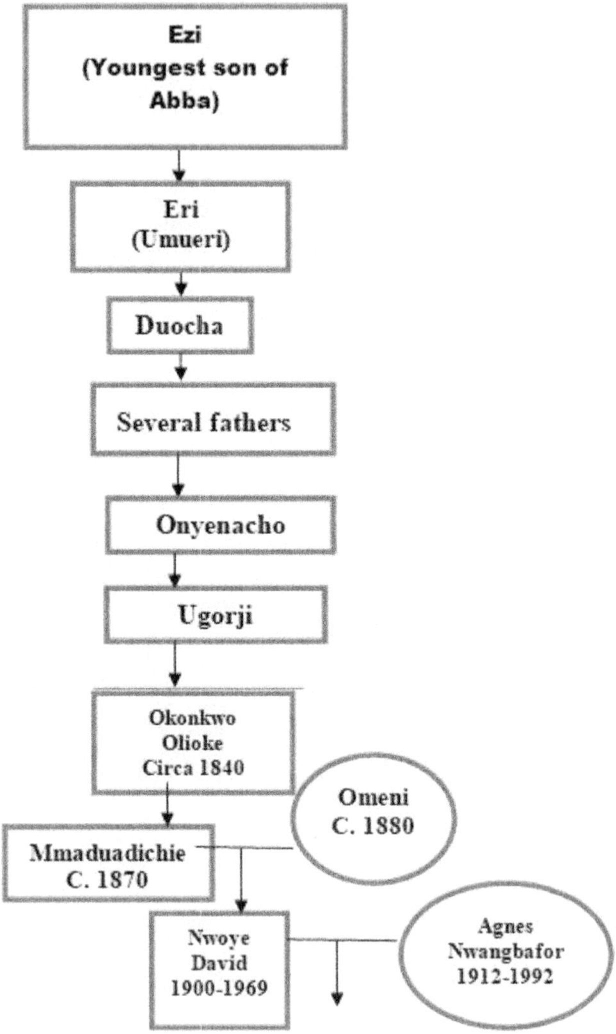

Please Turn Over

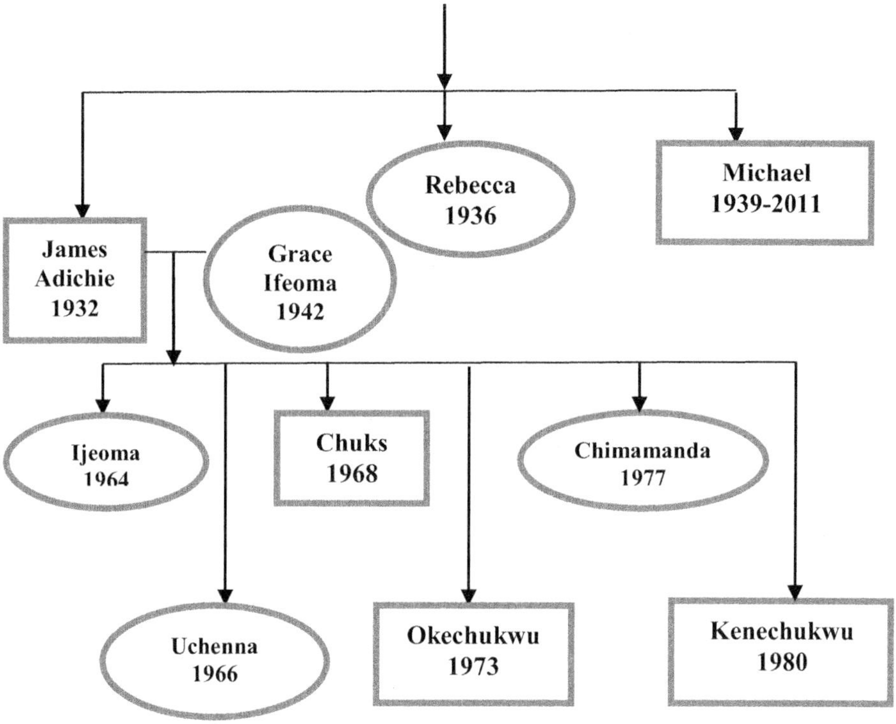
Rebecca
1936
Michael
1939-2011
James
Adichie
1932
Grace
Ifeoma
1942
Ijeoma
1964
Chuks
1968
Chimamanda
1977
Uchenna
1966
Okechukwu
1973
Kenechukwu
1980

PROLOGUE

In a tribute on Professor James Nwoye Adichie, B.A. (Mathematics, London, 1960), Ph.D. (Statistics, Univ. of California. Berkeley 1966), Nigeria's first Professor of Statistics, written by Prof. Biyi Afonja and posted on the web on May 28, 2009, one learns that: "James Nwoye Adichie was born on March 1, 1932 in Abba, Njikoka Local Government Area of Anambra State. After passing the Advanced Level Certificate of Education ("A" level GCE) examinations in Pure Mathematics, English and Latin, he was admitted into the University College Ibadan (UCI) now the University of Ibadan (UI) in 1957 to read mathematics. In those days when the UCI was a college of the University of London and was the only university institution in Nigeria, it was a remarkable achievement for a student to be admitted into the College. He graduated B.A. Mathematics of the University of London in 1960 among the top three students in a class of 13. At that time a student was awarded the B.A. degree if his/her A-Level subject combination included arts subjects in addition to the mathematics subject, and the B.Sc. degree if his/her subjects combination consisted of mathematics and science subjects"…

It is important to grasp the Adichie tempo for brilliance and determination, and to do so, let us go back one whole generation:

In 1900AD when James's father, Nwoye David (1900-1969) was born, life in Umueri hamlet was entirely one of a breezy village affair. The military preparations by the British colonial master to crush the Aro slave network, was in the local news before it was achieved two years later. In the meantime, there was a sustained lucrative interest in kidnapping young people for material gains. It is in this eerie environment in the centenary year 1900 that the baby boy Nwoye David was born to Maduadichie by his wife, Omeni. The boy's birth was coming at about two years after his only sister, named Mgbeke who died just before her second birthday. The name Nwoye, meant that he was born on Oye market day in the traditional Igbo four-day market week while Mgbeke meant that the sister was born on Eke market day. Nwoye was later baptized as David into the Christian faith (This was many years later).

As a child, Nwoye David looked sickly and seemed like one about to die. But providence had other plans for the Maduadichies as the boy was turning two. Being an only son, his mother, Omeni was almost inconsolable, but picked up the challenge with her firm character, to the admiration of the Umueri family and beyond to the wider Eziabba village and from there to the other villages of Abba town, now in Njikoka Local Government Area of Anambra State. Because Maduadichie left her no wealth, she decided to get clay from a faraway quarry within reach of a nearby riverside which she sold to enable her feed the sickly Nwoye David.

James' uncles, the Maduadichie half brothers, all lived together before James' father Nwoye died (1969) but the maintenance of cordiality was a mountainous task that had to be grappled with for the following reason. One fateful day in 1907(?), David's mother, widowed Omeni, went about her daily chores as every mother would. Her son, Nwoye, was left alone to play. It was just as if a plan had been hatched many moons before that fateful day; for calculatingly, kidnappers were waiting for action. Supposedly through insider information, a cue was set. Omeni's absence from her hut was the cue. Her liveliness made her absence conspicuous, inasmuch as the absence of the sound she made pounding foofoo, peeling melon, singing folk songs or teasing her sickly son was there for the prompting. But she was within hearing distance, only out of sight and somewhere at a corner of Maduadichie's compound. Thus, that day, the waiting kidnappers leapt over the low walls and made straight for Omeni's small hut where Nwoye David was. Upon sighting the little boy, they grabbed him and bolted away. Safely camouflaged in a plantation of banana behind the compound, the kidnappers blindfolded and gagged Nwoye before he would have the presence of mind to cry out for his mother. In this state, Nwoye was taken straight to a house in Awkuzu, a neighbouring town.

When Omeni discovered her son was missing, she went literarily mad with despair creating so much furore in Abba town that even the eight gods of Abba were not spared, as Omeni hassled their priests to no ends. The shrines of these gods became replete with Omeni's offerings, supplications and terrible tears that brought a hush in the town: everyone looked about for fear of the unknown, neighbours huddled together, waiting for the end, and no one dared raise a false hope or give off an unconcerned air. Just as people were contemplating how best to safeguard the town from kidnappers, so also they cower in fear of the repercussions of what had happened already.

But the finger of God is sure on Nwoye David. An unusual stance appeared in the affairs of the slave dealers. One by one, they took a look at the sickly Nwoye huddled in their house and decided he was not worth much. The patron in charge of the kidnappers' fortress summoned the kidnapers who brought Nwoye and ordered them to take him back quickly. After due consultations with so-and-so at Umueri, Nwoye was taken back to the banana plantation at night and left amongst the large banana leaves, still blindfolded, gagged and bound. Even though Nwoye looked sickly, he had the will to survive; he managed to untie himself and proceeded to remove the gag, working on it all night until early the next morning, when he was able to call out to his mother. Omeni was in her hut and was sure she heard the voice of her son. Despite the fear of being kidnapped herself, Omeni sprang up and grabbed her *Mmaekwu* (kitchen knife) and leapt with it to the outside, charging carefully into the banana plantation. When Nwoye was within sight, Omeni froze and was filled with uncontainable joy as she picked the boy and held him to herself. She washed Nwoye clear of the filth of his odysseys, and with lobes of kola nuts and her knife, she went immediately to the shrines of her eight gods and thanked them profusely, keeping Nwoye within her sight. It was no wonder then that as Nwoye David grew up, he saw before him the punishment settling like a cloud of locusts on people whom he believed were responsible for his travail. He impressed the divine intervention in his life upon his son, James, and upon his son's children who bear the name *Adichie* (People who replenish).

In the 1920s, when there was a quiet dignified village life at Umueri hamlet of Eziabba village and not many Abba people cared about going to school, Nwoye had the rare opportunity of going to Primary (or Elementary) school for two years. He would have continued, but for lack of support. Nevertheless, he benefited from going to school insofar as his level of education qualified him to get employed at the United Africa Company (UAC), Sapele, as a Clerk, recording the number of palm kernel bags each labourer carried into or out of the warehouse. It was a breakthrough – twilight of the Western way of life into which his son, James, was born.

CHAPTER ONE:
ROOTS AND CHILDHOOD

Our story begins at Abba town in the present Njikoka Local Government Area (LGA) of Anambra State, Nigeria, where James Nwoye Adichie was born on 1st March, 1932 into the family of Mr. Nwoye David Adichie of Umueri Quarters, Eziabba village of Abba and Nwangbafor Agnes Ekwenugo of Iruezeukwu Quarters, Igbuala village IfiteDunu in Dunukofia LGA of Anambra State. Originally, the town of Abba was made up of nine villages, but because of the frequent inter-village wars that were rampant before the arrival of Christianity in the second half of the 19th C, five out of the nine villages were sacked. Presently in the 21st C, there are four villages that make up Abba town: they are Ire, Amabor, Okpuloji and Eziabba. In cognizance of this vital part of the Abba memory, the sons and daughters of the town still refer to it as *Abba eboteghete,* that is, Abba of nine villages.

James as a child grew up in the serene environment of Abba with sturdy palm trees flung around its farm land reserves and a cluster of six surrounding communities, namely: Ukpo in the East, Awkuzu in the West, Ukwulu in the North, Ifitedunu in the South and South-West, Nawgu and Enugu-Agidi in the North-East. Towns that make up the present Njikoka Local Government Area of Anambra State are as follows: Abba, Abagana, Nimo on the one part as Umu-Owelle Clan and Enugwu-Ukwu, Enugwu-Agidi, Nawfia on the other part as Umu-Nri Clan (see Abba map). James was exposed to the rich cultural legacy of Abba, among which was the *Ede Opoto* festival and the *IwaJi* (New Yam) festival that featured, among other entertainments, masquerades, acrobatic dancers and farmers competition. James was also exposed to Christmas and Easter associated with the coming of Christianity.

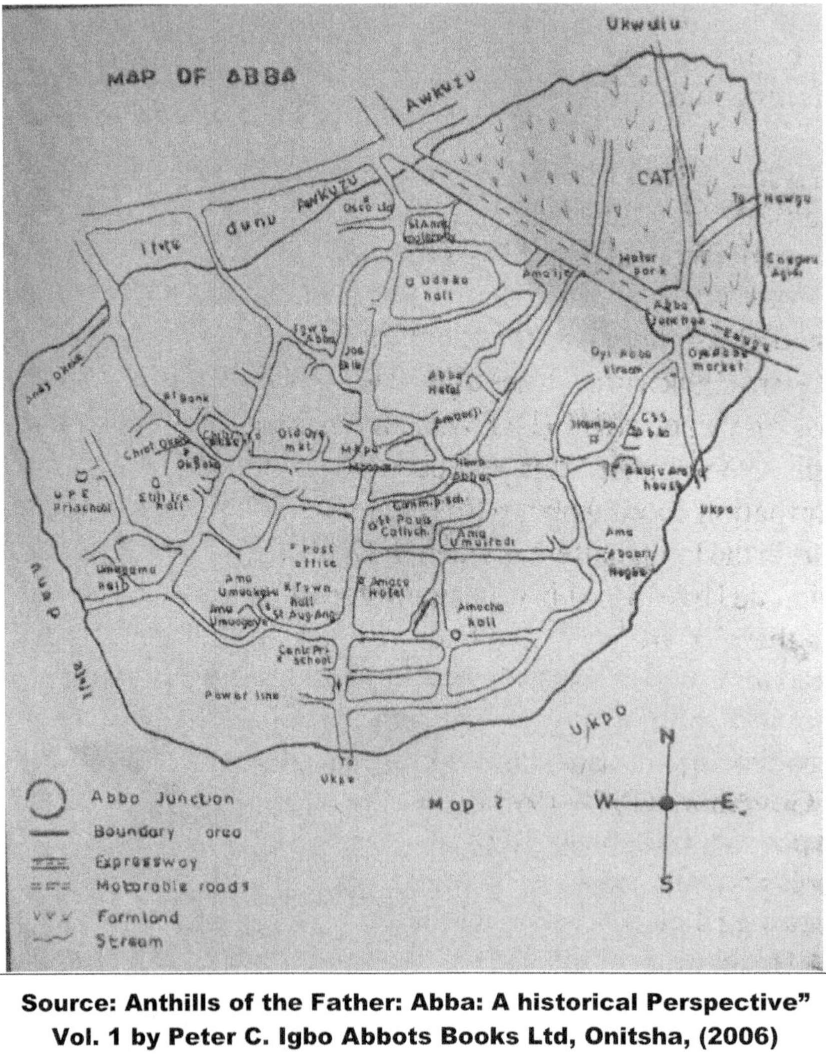

Source: Anthills of the Father: Abba: A historical Perspective" Vol. 1 by Peter C. Igbo Abbots Books Ltd, Onitsha, (2006)

Christianity came humbly to the heart of Igbo land as part of the British Trade Vessel called the *Dayspring,* which came up River Niger and anchored at Onitsha on July 27,1857. Amongst those onboard the ship were the Captain (Dr.) Baikie (a white naturalist whom the Igbo subsequently called *Bekee*) and Reverend Samuel Ajayi Crowther, a freed ordained Yoruba slave from Freetown Sierra Leone, who had successfully led the first1854 Christian Mission to Badagry in Yoruba land. There was also, Reverend John C Taylor, a grandson of freed Igbo slave who spoke the *Isuama* Igbo language, and a group of catechists. They all came with a mandate from the Church Missionary Society (CMS) to establish the Niger Mission (Crowder, 1978: 132) (Dike 1957: 10) (Crowther & Taylor, 1859). When *Dayspring* landed at Onitsha, it was immediately surrounded by security-conscious indigenes. After much diplomatic efforts, the foreigners were led by Oduche, a kingsman, to Okosi, the traditional ruler of Onitsha, through whose influence the Mission gained the trust of a section of Onitsha people. A mission house was erected in a land donated by an anonymous poor man and as early as August 1857, thirty Onitsha boys had become familiar with the first two letters of the English alphabet, courtesy of Reverend JC Taylor. A girls' school began a year later (Nwabara, 1977:49). From Onitsha, missionary work spread inwards. A church house of the Roman Catholic Mission (RCM) was established in the same Onitsha in 1886. A CMS church was dedicated in 1883 at Obosi by Crowther, who had already been made the Bishop of the

West Equatorial Africa in 1864. Christianity coupled with trade moved like wild fire into the Igbo hinterland.

Decades later, in 1917, a returnee slave from Port Harcourt came back to Abba. He began to worship at the CMS church at Abagana with his West Indian wife. Many people followed him, including Nwoye David. Since there was no church in Abba at the time, the converts naturally continued to go to Abagana. Later, in 1920, the RCM was founded at Abba, and, it was in this Church which Nwoye David helped found at Abba that he got married to his wife, Nwagbafor Agnes Ekwenugo, on June 4, 1929. Three years later on March 1, 1932, his first son, Nwoye Anagbalumnkpu Adichie was born. On August 1, 1932, the child was baptized and named James. Now, names were mostly bestowed on children, not necessarily by their parents, but more often than not, by the elders. The elders chose names which reflected the circumstances of the birth of a child. James' first name, Nwoye, meant a child born on *Oye* market day. His second name, Anagbalumnkpu, meant a loud prayer or supplication to *Ana* (the earth deity) for an emergent help offered to not only a new couple but also an entire hamlet, in this case, Umueri, in ensuring that a male child was born in the new home of the new couple.

Within the first six months of his life. James had bouts of cerebral malaria which continued until he was about three years old. This condition, coupled with yaws, was very distressing to his parents. The fever sometimes made him hallucinate or see apparitions. One of these apparitions, which was called "Etipọmpọm", would jeer at him. According to James Adichie (2012:1), "...my mother, in response to my distress cry, would throw sticks, kitchen knives, ladles and brooms in the direction of Etipọmpọm...." James' father would carry him on his bicycle and rush to the village square where a doctor visited once a month to give drugs and injections to sick people. His mother would take him to "Nweke Mmili's house" who would administer anti-malarial drugs and other local herbs to James. Fortunately, God answered the prayers of the distressed parents and the fever bouts subsided with time so that James was able to start school.

The training that James received from his grandmother was interesting. The old-and-knowing woman was living with the Adichies in the same compound. She knew that the early days of sickness may set James up for being over-pampered. So to curtail the doting force of habit coming from one and all towards James, she taught him to sweep the house, throw away ashes collected in the kitchen hearth and to do other sundry chores which his mates were doing in their homes. James recalls in Adichie (2012:2): "My grandmother was afraid that my parents might prefer to do these chores themselves, so that I would be entirely free to play, eat and go to school. She called that 'Nzuto' [spoiling or over pampering].My mother, obviously did not like my grandmother to send me on small errands, but grandma overruled my mother's sensibilities. So I soon joined other boys of my age to play and hunt for butterflies, crickets, and lizards. We knew how to distinguish the male from the female goats, sheep, dogs and other domestic animals that were in every compound. Because my sister was four years my junior, I even knew how to scrub the floor of our house (typically a female chore)".

James was a precocious child. He had great interest in going to school as soon as he was old enough to comprehend formal learning. And his father was willing to sponsor him in school, having seen the importance of education himself.

But it was a near disaster that it was only James that had that privilege of going to school amongst his contemporaries, which did not go down well with his age grade. One of the traditions in Umueri hamlet was to have certain age grades sweep *Ama-eze (*the village square) where people gathered for resort in the evenings and where important village meetings were held. James' age grade was required to sweep the village square every morning of an *Oye* market day, but James always got ready for school every week day, irrespective of whether it fell on *Oye* or not. This situation not only set him up for ridicule but also embittered members of his age grade who labored with brooms to sweep the square while he took off to school! It did not help that he strolled into the *Ama-eze* in the evenings like everyone else for *egwuọnwa* (moonlight play). He would have been beaten up but for the fact that a man always took him to school.

James had a head start in learning acrobatics which were part of his school activities. His skill in wrestling, running and fist-fighting was honed much more than those of the members of his age grade. From 1935 to

1936, he began kindergarten at RCM school, Abba, doing what was called "Ntakara" (pupils who eat bean cake) or "NdiNwui" in onomatopoeic expression of the Igbo alphabets taught at such level. In 1937, he began Infant I at RCM school, Abba too. By 1938, he had concluded Infant II. In 1939, he quickly began Standard I at the same RCM school, Abba in a place believed to be Eziabba land, where the first Roman Catholic Mission (RCM) Church in Abba was located.

Unfortunately, Standard II was scrapped at the school. Consequently, in 1940, James had to go along with all others who had passed Standard I to St. Raphael's RCM School, Awkuzu for his Standard II. He attended this school for four years.

Within that time, his old conflict with members of his age grade had gotten to a head. They had taken measures to make him either pay the stipulated fine of one penny each day he failed to participate in sweeping the *ama-eze* or stop coming to the square for *egwuọnwa.* Because they could not implement the fine option, they resorted to chasing him out of the square each time they sighted him around it. Some of them regarded him as "different" from them. Some would not talk to him. As he put it in Adichie (2012:3), "The elders (my father's group) got to know of this 'expulsion' verdict passed on me, and reacted angrily against the *ama-eze* boys. So I could walk past *ama-eze*, I could sometimes (but not as frequent as I used to do) come to *egwuọnwa,* though with trepidation"

When they found that the harassment did not work, the children reported James to their seniors. The mischief-seeking senior boys naturally supported them. They would give James a scowl and a painful banter like "Chekwalu nu nwata akwukwo ka ogafelu, o sua oyibo iga anu? (Please allow the school boy to pass. If he speaks English, will you understand?)" On a fateful day, James' father sent him on an errand and to ensure he returned early as it was almost nightfall, his father had given him his bicycle for use. As James was riding back to Umueri on the pathway that cut through the *amaeze*, he noticed that a number of the senior boys were loitering in the square. They stopped him and forced him down the bicycle. Then they told him that he must wrestle with one NwankwoNwade who was his age mate. The boys immediately called out Nwankwo whose family home was very close to the square. He ran out to meet the group. They told him that James had been boasting that he could defeat him in wrestling, even though James did no such thing. The accusation was designed to get Nwankwo worked up to frenzy and challenge James immediately and the trick worked. Incidentally, James dreaded Nwankwo because of his bully attitude even though they were age mates. So when Nwankwo rushed at him, he avoided his grip. As he was running away from Nwankwo, his mind worked up into a conflict. He wanted to get away but a part of him strongly persuaded him to turn and face Nwankwo and engage him in wrestling. Fortunately, he was sufficiently persuaded to challenge Nwankwo. Utilizing his skill of athletics and stamina, he was able to maneuver Nwankwo until he held him to his hips and then in one powerful shove had him crashing to the ground. Just as Nwankwo got to the ground, defeated, so also all his praise singers became aghast. They stopped egging him on and silently came up to them and lifted James up by the hand. After that seeming duel, his peers never pressured James anymore about sweeping the amaeze.

James' father was a very stoic man. He made sure James grew up a disciplined child. He would not allow him to talk to girls in compromising ways. Sometimes, he stayed up to four days before he would ask James who the girl he talked to four days earlier was. This gave the question some weight. At a younger age, James usually ran away from his father's cane. But then when his father declared that when he had done with running, he would come back home, James would have no choice but return slowly back to the house.

About this time also, James' mates were getting initiated into the masquerade cult. His father, who was a devout Catholic, felt that it was normal also to integrate James into some aspects of the customs of the land. He quietly went to the initiation committee and paid the requisite dues for James' initiation into the masquerade cult. These included money for mask handlers' food (*isu nni mmanwu*) and yams etc. He did not need to let James know of it. On the day of initiation, James' father called about four of the initiation committee members and told them, "Nne nu James, dulu nu ya, mma nu ya mmo" meaning, "This is James, take him and initiate him into the masquerade cult" That was it.

Adichie (2012:4) reveals, "Usually, initiation was a tough climb. The [prospective] initiates would be beaten, falsely accused of theft or felony etc. Each time they tried to deny these accusations or establish their innocence, they would be beaten by both human beings and masquerades that had gathered at the initiation point. For me, I didn't experience any of the ordeals of initiation. My father's clout probably simplified things for me. I got it on a platter of gold".

Back to James' education, by 1943, what happened at Abba, also happened at Awkuzu: the top class, which was Standard six, was scrapped. During the promotional examinations for admission into Standard Six anywhere else, only three pupils passed. Two pupils had to repeat Standard Five with other pupils because they could not find a place willing to admit them for Standard Six. James proceeded to Nimo for his Standard Six. Now there was another school at Abagana which had Standard Six and was nearer home than Nimo. But because the school was owned by the Church Missionary Society (CMS), James dared not go there. The CMS and RCM were arch-rivals within South-eastern Nigeria at the time. The bad blood got to the extent that pupils who were graduating from RCM schools never got admitted into CMS schools for further studies. The two were like oil and water that never mixed. Therefore, James had to seek admission into St. Bonaventure RCM School at Nimo in 1944.

Adichie (2012:3) reminisces, "During our childhood days, Catholics and non-Catholics kept to themselves; there was little or no communication between them. This state of affairs affected my perception about Catholic and non-Catholic schools, hymns, songs, dances and other social events in the town. The aspect of this religious divide was how we (my parents and I) were denied participation in non-Catholic wedding ceremonies (even eating fried yams or drinking Fanta [soft drink], being what we looked forward to in a wedding). Similarly, non-Catholics would dare not come to a Catholic wedding reception, not to mention going to a Catholic church where the wedding was being celebrated. Minor clashes also occurred between Catholic and non-Catholic pupils as each side sang songs in derision of the other, e.g., 'Father oli bread, father afu-onu kpom kpom' or 'selemans selu ikpukpu ukwa' [This respectively means, 'Father, eater of bread, Father with the scraggy beard' and the onomatopoeic 'CMS draw out the husks of breadfruits']. However, the situation has now changed. There is free communication between the RCM and CMS adherents in Abba".

At Nimo, it was difficult for James to find accommodation. From Abba to Nimo was about five miles and at that tender age of twelve, James could only manage to do the rounds for five days and became overwhelmed with the stress.

Nwoye David, his father, had to solve the problem fast. He quickly visited a man, Mr. J.U. Ekwunife, who was teaching at Agulu which was closer to Nimo. He appealed to him to help him find accommodation for his son. Ekwunife had to oblige because he had served David as a child. James concluded his primary education while living with a Nimo family as arranged by Mr. Ekwunife.

When his final examinations results were out, it was discovered that James had taken first position in the entire Adazi parish at the time. The then Adazi parish of the RCM included Nimo, Awkuzu and Abagana.

Unfortunately, Abba town was no longer part of the Adazi parish of the RCM, but had been included into Dunukofia parish. So, James and his father had to proceed to Dunukofia to see how the young boy would gain admission to college, instead of at St. Anthony's Teacher Training College Onitsha, as was the missionary educational policy at the time.

At this time, James was able to meet Reverend Father Iwene Tansi who was a priest at Dunukofia. His impression of Tansi was that though he stuttered, he was a remarkably pious man who did not allow that seeming defect to get in his way. While he sought for admission into College, James had to begin teaching at the Parish. Because he was thirteen years at the time, he was considered underage since the minimum age for teachers was fourteen. Therefore, he was asked to teach kindergarteners. He was paid half a penny which was the equivalent of sixteen cowries. Having attained the minimum teaching age in 1946, James was posted to St. Raphael's in Awkuzu to teach Standard II. The next year, he gained admission into the Africa College which was founded by Mr. Peter Chukwurah, an Abatete man. The school was situated in a large expanse of field which had many hewn tree stumps. The tree trunks obtained from there were used for the new three-classroom-school. The school was not fenced and it was at the back of the Christ the King College at Onitsha. As part of school punishment, students were often asked to go cut the tree stumps in the precincts of the school. It was possible, that James' set were the pioneer students of the College.

It was the custom of the college to enter students in class three so that within four years, those students could have acquired the Senior Cambridge Examination Certificate. Other schools such as the Dennis Memorial Grammar School had no such quick route. James studied in Class Three and Four and left in 1948 after sitting for and passing his Junior Cambridge Examinations. He went back to teaching at Awkuzu – this time he was asked to teach primary four pupils. This was from January to September 1949.

Right from his days at the Africa College, James had it in mind to sit for the Senior Cambridge Examinations. So he was already studying privately for it when a Reverend Father who was in charge of secondary schools and some primary schools in the Onitsha Catholic Diocese saw his results. Incidentally, a new school was opened in Lagos by the colonial government. It was the Yaba Technical Institute which was housed in the old Yaba Higher College. The Reverend Father recommended that James should acquire technical education. The man helped him to gain admission into the Technical Institute Yaba (T.I.Y.) to do a two-year Manual Training Instructor's Course.

CHAPTER TWO:
HIGHER EDUCATION AND JOBS

James arrived Lagos on Friday, October 13, 1949. Within the TIY, there were three modules of study: (a) The Junior Technical (same as Secondary/ Technical School) open to candidates having only First School Leaving Certificate; (b) The Manual Training Instructor's Course (Open to candidates having at least Government Class IV certificate); (c) Handcraft Training Instructor's Course (open only to candidates having Senior Cambridge School Certificate). In the Manual Training Instructor's Course, James Adichie studied Physics, Chemistry, Maths, Metal Work, Wood Work and Technical Drawing in addition to Teaching Methods. He passed the final Diploma examinations and gained the Diploma with an aggregate grade of A, in June 1951. In July 1951, James secured a job of teaching handicraft to teachers in training at St. Anthony's Teacher's Training College at Agulu (in Anambra State).

In December 1951, James having left the T.I.Y., was then free to take the Senior Cambridge School Certificate Examination for which he had been preparing through the Wolsey Hall Oxford, Correspondence Course.

He took the examination at Lagos Centre II (for private candidates) and passed in Grade I, with exemption from London Matriculation. James stayed in St. Anthony's College, Agulu, teaching up until 1953, when he resigned his teaching job and switched to the Civil Service. He secured a job in the Eastern Nigeria

Ministry of Health, as a Sanitary Inspector in training, and was admitted into the School of Hygiene at Aba (now in Abia State). His independent and assertive spirit showed itself in student unionism at this stage of his life such that his superiors thought he was arrogant. The Doctor in charge of the school sent him and one Ewelukwa off for small pox campaigns to Agbani and other areas in Enugu State as a way of punishment. Upon graduating from the School of Hygiene in July 1955, James had to still go for these campaigns as part of a sanitary job.

When the sanitary team got to Oji River Local Government Area Secretariat, a remote place at the time, they had problems of hunger and difficult transportation from one place to another. Sometimes, James solved the problem of hunger by eating coconut. At Agbani, they went to solve the problem of small pox in a village now near Four-Corner in today's Enugu capital city. It was here that James discovered that females also answered the name, Nwankwo. This is a name that is commonly given to Igbo males. Before he got to know of this, James had already submitted some statistical reports of mortality rates which gave more male figures than they were in reality because he erroneously thought that some names of people who had died from the disease as called out to him by the villagers were those of males. It did not help that obtaining such reports from the indigenes required careful measures as the disease was highly infectious. James and his colleague wore rain boots into which they tucked the hems of their trousers. They also wore protective caps and lived in a hut. Despite these measures, they still got bitten by sand flies coming from the bush. The team obtained the mortality reports by summoning a man into their quarantined hut where they questioned him for figures. By the time James became aware of his errors in figures, not a few reports had gone in thereby causing some conflicts of reports as the information from the team got compared by the sanitary officers.

The man who initially alerted the team of the small pox problem was a somewhat manipulative fellow. He would gather his fellow villagers and wrongly inform them that if they brought goats and other gifts, they would not be inoculated in places in their hands that would spell doom for them. Of course, the entire gifts were diverted by the man. When James got wind of this subterfuge, he accosted the man and tried to make him see the foolishness of his actions. The man was peeved. At that time, James was sitting for GCE advanced level at Aba. So, he left for Aba frequently. The man knew of his travels so he felt he could use this information against him. He went and reported to the Sanitary Officers stationed at Agbani that James hardly stayed in his duty post but traveled about, especially to Aba. Routinely, sanitary officers gave regular reports to the Medical Officer of Health (MOH) in charge of the small pox campaign. He was a man from Malta. The then Chief Medical Officer of Health was Dr. Onyemelukwe. Now, when the sanitary officers gave the report of James' supposed illegal itinerary to the Malta man, he worked up to frenzy and stormed the local railway. He was determined to find out the truth of the matter by himself. He met a railway man who changed rail tracks and asked him to get details of James' itinerary from the trains' manifests. The man went through the manifests and reported to the Malta man that it was Enugu, not Aba, that James had traveled to. The Maltese summoned James and asked him where he was on a certain day as supposedly recorded in the manifest, James replied that he had gone to Enugu. It was a matter of hygiene for all the sanitary officers to go to Enugu for their laundry at certain periods of time. Despite that every other person had regularly gone to Enugu for this, the Maltese thought that he could still give James a query for traveling. He quickly drafted one, handed it over to James, stormed to his car and zoomed off. A part of the query read, "It is on record that you travelled down Port Harcourt way.... You left your beat without permission.... You have twenty four (24) hours to explain why disciplinary action should not be taken against you...." (Adichie, 2013a).

The railway man the Maltese had met called James and told him how he had been questioned. He then informed James that the Maltese had no right whatsoever to grant him an off-day whenever James needed one and that there was not supposed to be permission for the routine Enugu laundry round. Bolstered by this information, James wrote four pages in response to the query. He wrote that as a matter of hygiene, he needed no permission to launder the clothes as small pox was highly infectious. He observed that the MOH had right to give a query when necessary but had no right in trying to take a disciplinary action against him. Upon reading James' reply, the MOH saw the point and quickly intercepted the query before it could get to the CMOH.

James passed his Advanced level GCE in four papers, namely, Pure and Applied Mathematics, English Literature and Latin. Of course, he wanted to leave the sanitary job. When his results came out, he left the job and went to teach at Okongwu Memorial School at Nnewi. The school's name memorialized Nnodu Okongwu, a man from Nnewi.

After a while, James left Okongwu Memorial School and went to teach at New Bethel College at Onitsha sometime in the mid 1950's. he was at New Bethel College until June 1957. A few weeks later, he gained admission into the University College, Ibadan (UCI) through direct entry to study Mathematics. In those days, the UCI was a college of the University of London and was the only university institution in Nigeria, it was a remarkable achievement for a student to be admitted into the College at the time. One of his classmates was Biyi Afonja, who later became a Professor of Statistics shortly after James Adichie became the first Professor of Statistics. James' experiences at Ibadan were interesting. He had the privilege of having Professor Chike Obi teach him Mathematics. Professor Chike Obi was then a young and dynamic academic politician. He usually arrived late for lectures because of his tight schedules. One day, while rushing through a lecture, he noticed Afonja glancing at his wristwatch just as if to say the lecturer should mind that time was running or that he should just go. This gesture infuriated Chike Obi and he was almost literally down on Afonja, scolding him fervently for trying to time him. Later, Chike Obi met Adichie within the University campus and thinking he was Afonja, began to reprimand him again. Chike Obi was a forceful and principled man. Adichie was horrified. He tried to point out to Chike Obi that he was not the student who glanced at his wristwatch in class. Upon realizing his mistake, Chike Obi began to call both Adichie and Afonja brothers. Afonja was very brilliant, however playful, in class. He made his classmates reel with laughter after pointing out the idiosyncrasies of their lecturers. For instance, he penned down the number of times their female Maths Professor said "am", which was another way of saying "em" usually spoken subconsciously when one is thinking of what next to say. When the poor woman left the class, Afonja would come to the black board and reveal how many times she mentioned the monosyllable, making his classmate release their stress in raucous laughter. He was to become the second and very popular Professor of Statistics in Nigeria, a feat reserved only for champions.

Adichie graduated B.A. Mathematics (Pure and Advanced) of the University of London in 1960 among the top three students in a class of 13. The two other students who got high grades were Biyi Afonja and Charles Sowunmi. At that time a student was awarded the B.A. degree if his/her A-Level subject combination included arts subjects in addition to the mathematics subject; and the B.Sc degree if his/her subjects combination consisted of mathematics and science subjects. The Mathematics programme in University College, Ibadan (UCI) graciously accommodated only a bit of statistics. Out of the eight Mathematics papers for the degree examination, only two contained one or two questions in Statistics. Neither Professor Adichie nor his colleagues had any compelling attraction for the statistics component of the mathematics programme. The course of lectures in Statistics were, in effect, largely ignored or at best merely audited with detached interest. So they completed their undergraduate programme with scant romance with statistics. But this appeared to be all the freedom that destiny would accord Prof. Adichie in the choice of Statistics as a career.

CHAPTER THREE: BEGINNINGS OF CAREER, MARRIAGE, POSTGRADUATE EDUCATION AND THE NIGERIAN CIVIL WAR

The first emphatic action by destiny to give him not only a seat in the Statistics train but also a hand on the steering was when, on finishing his University education at U.C.I., he quickly got a job in the Central Bank of Nigeria near Tinubu Square in Lagos in 1960. Here, he was posted to the Research section of the Bank and he now had to use that same Statistics that he, as a brilliant undergraduate student of mathematics, distanced himself from. It is to the credit of the University education then that the sense of enquiry of students was well primed. One of his first assignments in the Research Unit of the Central Bank was to package a paper on the Nigerian economy (Adichie, 2013d). This was a challenge which even young economists and Statisticians faced with trepidation then. Trained to be thorough in whatever he did, Prof Adichie girded his loins and prepared to deliver excellent result. He read voraciously anything he could lay his hands on in Statistics and Economics. Eventually, the report which he turned in became the only one found worthy to be specially published by the Bank as its Occasional Report No.1. This was because of the depth of research in it. Spectacular as this was, it was still not enough to persuade the young graduate to stay on in the Bank. He felt that as a mathematician working in an area of economics, the future of his career may not be as rosy as it appears then when bright graduates of economics or statistics became employed. Because of this he had started nursing the desire to resign from CBN. When, as soon as the degree results of the University were released and he passed in flying colours, he requested to be allowed to resign. His boss who had developed a liking for him refused. But he had made up his mind to leave the Bank and its Statistics and its Economics. Even CBN, the envy of job seekers, with all its flashy setting could not hold him back. For destiny had not finished with him.

When the young and purposeful graduate was eventually and reluctantly allowed to leave CBN, another irony set in. He was now out of job (having left CBN because of Statistics). Ironically, the next job that came his way was employment still as a Statistician in the Federal Office of Statistics, the home of that same statistics that he seemed unwilling to associate with. It is interesting to quickly point out here that much later in life and as a Professor of Statistics, he was appointed Chairman by the Federal Government to reorganize this important Parastatal (Adichie, 2013d). As he hung on to the FOS appointment, he was seriously looking for a job elsewhere. It is germane to note here that Adichie bought his first car, an Opel, while he was working at FOS.

Soon what seemed like an opportunity for the type of job he wanted came. He was given appointment as a Mathematics teacher in Nigerian College of Arts, Science and Technology (NCAST) located in Enugu. It looked as if the chicken had come home to roost. It seemed as if it was now a square peg in a square hole. But wait again because what happened next seemed to suggest that no one can and indeed should try to out maneuver his or her destiny. For no sooner than he took up the appointment as a Mathematics Teacher in the College, the College itself was closed for good on the order of the then Government of Nigeria. His employment in the Nigerian College lasted only from December, 1960 to August, 1961. Yet again, Adichie was out of work. But this destiny that has been trying to shape his future did not allow him to stay for long without work. So another irony set in.

University of Nigeria opened its gates to students in 1960. One of the Departments it began with was the Department of Mathematics, Statistics and Astronomy. The then Head of Department, Professor P.C. Chaudhuri, was desirous of opening up the Statistics programme of the Department. The Department got to know about one young graduate, J.N. Adichie residing in Enugu. Arrangements were quickly made and a staff of the Department was sent to Enugu to interview him. The interview took place in the sitting room of his residence in the campus of the now defunct Nigerian College. It seemed that the interview was a formality; for the quintessential capabilities of the candidate had preceded him to the Department at Nsukka. And so it was that our respected Professor (then, of course, Mr J.N. Adichie) got appointment in the University of Nigeria, Nsukka as an Assistant Lecturer in September, 1961. He also acquired a small flat at the hilly Elias Avenue within the Senior Staff Quarters. If he thought he was now into a career in Mathematics in the University he was making a mistake because destiny had not finished with him. At the University of Nigeria, he was given assignment to start the Statistics programme of the Department and to teach Statistics. This seemed to be the ultimate irony. He was actually summoned by Professor P.C. Chaudhuri into his office. When he appeared, the Indian brought down old tomes of Statistics books from his shelf. He asked Adichie to read these books in order to get acquainted with Statistics so that he would teach it to students in the Department from the following week. At first Adichie was not keen. In fact he rejected the proposal out rightly. Then, Professor P.C. Chaudhuri said firmly, "If you do not want to teach the course, then you don't have the job"

Of course, Adichie who did not want to lose the job quickly replied, "Please, I think I am ready now to handle the course!" (Adichie, 2013c).

It would appear that Professor J.N. could not run fast enough to escape from Statistics. I dare say this was the only race he would not win. *When God has a plan for you, He brings it to completion in a way that is beyond understanding*.

During this time also, the young James Adichie was already thinking of settling down. By act of Providence, he had met and fallen in love with the very beautiful and sociable Grace Ifeoma J.P. from the Odigwe family. Grace Ifeoma was then a young twenty-year old lady. They were married on April 15, 1963. They also moved to a small verandaed bungalow at Odim Street. The house had flowers in front of the porch. Shortly afterwards, Prof. J.N. Adichie (now a permanent employee of the University of Nigeria, Nsukka) was sent to the University of California, Berkeley for a Ph.D in Statistics. His wife, Grace, had attended the Rosary High School, Enugu from 1956 to 1958, and the Queen of the Rosary College, Onitsha from 1959 to 1960, obtaining the West African School Certificate Division II in 1960. Thus, it was natural for her to proceed to Merit College, Oakland California, USA in 1964 in order to be near to her husband.

At the University of California, Berkeley, there was no mercy for a neophyte nor for the faint hearted. The standard is set and you either ship in or ship out. It was a tough life for the young James Adichie who at first seemed overwhelmed by the depth of lecture content, the speed of lecture delivery and the merciless expectations from the Department.

He saw himself in the midst of mostly Indian students who had acquired their Master's degrees already. They had a head start in Statistics. The first quiz that Adichie experienced was a terrible baptism of fire. Adichie (2013a) reveals, "Once a month, you are given a quiz. Conventionally, you read the exam question papers from beginning to the end. Then, you read it again to mark the questions you want to attempt. In my first quiz, I got zero".

This experience shook him so much that he scurried to his supervisor's office and blurted out that he wanted to go home. His supervisor, a very brilliant professor, encouraged James Adichie to stick on to Statistics and not to abandon ship and bolt for home. Without this strong motivation from his supervisor, James Adichie would have lost focus.

It is important to divagate a little to the intellectual background history or origins of the type of Statistics at the University of California, Berkeley. Adichie's supervisor was Erich Leo Lehmann (20 November 1917-12 September 2009). Erich Lehmann himself was supervised by Jerzy Splawa-Neyman (April 16, 1894 – August 5, 1981.

Erich Leo Lehmann was an American statistician, who contributed to statistical and nonparametric hypothesis testing. He is one of the eponyms of the Lehmann–Scheffé theorem and of the Hodges–Lehmann estimator of the median of a population. Lehmann obtained his MA in 1942 and his PhD (under Jerzy Neyman) in 1946, at the University of California, where he taught from 1942. His PhD was entitled, "Optimum Tests of a Certain Class of Hypothesis Specifying the Value of a Correlation Coefficient". During 1944–1945 he worked as an analyst for United States Air Force. He taught at Columbia University and at Princeton University during 1950–51, and then during 1951–1952 he was a visiting associate professor at Stanford University. He was an editor of "The Annals of Mathematical Statistics" and president of the Institute of

Mathematical Statistics, and a member of the American Academy of Arts and Sciences and the National Academy of Science. In 1997, on the occasion of his eightieth birthday, the department of statistics at the University of California at Berkeley created the Erich Lehmann Fund in Statistics to support the students of the department.

Jerzy Splawa-Neyman was the man who brought certain seriousness to statistics in the United States of America. He was a Polish American mathematician and statistician who spent most of his professional career at the University of California, Berkeley. Neyman was the first to introduce the modern concept of a confidence interval into statistical hypothesis testing. He was born into a Polish family in Bendery, Bessarabia in Imperial Russia, the fourth of four children of Czesław Spława-Neyman and Kazimiera Lutosławska. His family was Roman Catholic and Neyman served as an altar boy during his early childhood. Later, Neyman would become an agnostic. He began studies at Kharkov University in 1912, where he was taught by Russian probabilist Sergei Natanovich Bernstein. After he read "Lessons on the integration and the research of the primitive functions" by Henri Lebesgue, he was fascinated with measure and integration. In 1921, he returned to Poland in a program of repatriation of POWs after the Polish-Soviet War. He earned his Doctor of Philosophy degree at University of Warsaw in 1924 for a dissertation titled "On the Applications of the Theory of Probability to Agricultural Experiments". He was examined by Wacław Sierpiński and Stefan Mazurkiewicz, among others. He spent a couple of years in London and Paris on a fellowship to study statistics with Karl Pearson and Émile Borel. After his return to Poland he established the Biometric Laboratory at the Nencki Institute of Experimental Biology in Warsaw. He published many books dealing with experiments and statistics, and devised the way which the FDA tests medicines today. Neyman proposed and studied randomized experiments in 1923.

Furthermore, his paper "On the Two Different Aspects of the Representative Method: The Method of Stratified Sampling and the Method of Purposive Selection", given at the Royal Statistical Society on 19 June 1934, was the groundbreaking event leading to modern scientific sampling. He introduced the confidence interval in his paper in 1937. Another noted contribution is the Neyman-Pearson lemma, the basis of hypothesis testing. In 1938 he moved to Berkeley, where he worked for the rest of his life. Thirty-nine students received their Ph.D's under his advisorship. In 1966 he was awarded the Guy Medal of the Royal Statistical Society and three years later the (American) Medal of Science. He died in Oakland, California.It is in the context of this seriousness of statistics at Berkeley that the young Adichie found himself.

A winner is always a winner. When the going gets tough, the saying goes, the tough gets going. So it was that at Berkeley, Adichie started literally to learn Statistics from scratch. Some other students who were at Berkeley and also had Erich Leymann as their supervisor were Shulamith Gross (an Israeli, she later became the first PhD, while Adichie became the second PhD), Arthur Hoadley and Gouri Bhattacharyya. In the atmosphere of serious statistical learning and leanings, these students pushed ahead in their bid to emerge well-formed.

With the strong encouragement of his supervisor who guided him in understudying statistical courses, Adichie rolled up his sleeves, pulled himself out of a creeping and unhelpful frame of mind and quickly began to stamp his authority over the challenging academic environment. This was to the complete admiration of his supervisor. His composure and new approach to the challenge confronting him were excellent, his determination was exemplary and the results he produced were astounding and a delight. By dint of hard work, therefore, he transformed himself from a new comer in Statistics to a leader and pacesetter in a discipline that had seemed anathema to him. His brilliance was such that in his year of graduation, he was the second person to finish his PhD programme in that global centre of excellence in Statistics, the University of California where the movers and shakers in the world of Statistics were powering away on all cylinders. His 146-paged PhD thesis was entitled, *Nonparametric Inference in Linear Regression*. Prof. J.N. Adichie and Statistics have now become inexorably and inseparably bound together by destiny and by hard work; they have now become truly wedded.

Back to Nigeria, he became the first PhD holder in the field of Statistics in the country. What a marvel! It is this achievement, this spirit of doggedness, this cooperation with the force of destiny that is today being celebrated. On the celebration podium is an unrepentant Mathematician who through recourse to his innate abilities and prodded by the unseen hand of destiny has not only become an oracle but also the foremost advocate of Statistics

In June 1966, our man of the moment, our octogenarian, returned from USA with the proverbial Golden Fleece, a PhD in Statistics from a world class University. He took up the position waiting for him in the University of Nigeria. Between July 1966 and June 1973, he was in the Lecturer position. This is a period that spanned the Nigeria-Biafra war. His first assignment was to draw up a syllabus for the Statistics programme of the Department. He also designed a service course in Statistics for students of other programmes. By this he pioneered the creation of Statistics programme and set the tone and direction for the growth of statistics in the University. This assignment, executed all alone, was carried out with dedication and thoroughness. Upon approval of the Programme by Senate, he led a dedicated team of two younger lecturers in delivering the programme to students. Although his major area was Non-parametric Statistics, he also took on such other courses as Stochastic processes and probability theory. These he delivered in such a masterly and down to earth manner that it was always a joy to expect and audit his lectures. One of the authors of this biography (Prof. Peter I. Uche) is a proud beneficiary of his deep wisdom, his intellectual correctness and his fatherly disposition. Lecture notes in all his courses became a reference point for decades and for generations of students of Statistics. Students of the University who passed through him have been powering the growth of the nation with such sense of mission, confidence and insight" virtues learnt from the exemplary devotion of this quiet and unassuming genius, Prof. J.N. Adichie.

Unfortunately, the Nigerian Civil War interrupted the inchoate stage of the formation of a strong statistics tradition in the University of Nigeria. Prof. Adichie was settling down to watering the flower of Statistics in the University of Nigeria when tension began to build in the University campus. He had taught for only one session and was preparing for another one, following a brave convocation ceremony held the night of Friday, June 30, 1967 for the zero-hour graduates. This convocation was held at night because of fears of air raids from Nigerian planes if it were held the next morning as scheduled and widely publicized.

Any serious brief account of the roots of the war would include the first coup executed in Nigeria. For following the first coup of January 15, 1966 in which, circumstantially, mostly northern leaders were assassinated than were leaders of any other ethnic group in Nigeria, a huge wave of massacre of people of Eastern Nigeria began in Northern Nigeria. The perpetrators of the bloodletting were convinced, rather hurriedly, that the coup was executed by Igbos against northern leaders. Many Igbo people fled the North. There immediately followed a counter-coup on July 29, 1966, spearheaded by Northern officers in which the then Head of State, General JTU Aguiyi-Ironsi, an Igbo, was killed. A fresh wave of killings began in which also many Igbo military officers were gunned down by mutinous northern troops. Thousands of easterners began an exodus back home to Eastern Region. The influx was particularly high in September and October 1966, following the grave Kano massacre of Igbos on September 29. Many academics that were once in western universities such as University of Ibadan and University of Lagos mostly flooded into the University of Nigeria, Nsukka, the only such federal university in the east at the time. There were talks of an impending war between Eastern Nigeria (which adopted the name and flag of Biafra) and the rest of Nigeria. Every day, there were news releases and statements towards the eventuality of war by either the then Military Governor of Eastern Region, Lieut. Col. Odumegwu Ojukwu or by the Military Head of State of Nigeria, Lt. Col. Yakubu Gowon. For example, on March 14, 1967, 24 hours after Ojukwu said the East would secede if blockaded or attacked, the Head of State quickly warned that he would deal severely with the Eastern Region if it proceeded with secession plans. On May 30, 1967, Eastern Region seceded and Biafra was born. On July 6, 1967, Nigerian troops invaded Biafra, capturing Obollo town near Nsukka after some exchange of fire (Aneke, 2007:123).

Up until July 10, 1967, there was serious uncertainty as to when Nsukka and the University would be invaded by the Nigerian troops. Civil defense personnel were instructing people on how to defend themselves just in case there were air raids. As the Nigerian troops advanced, Biafran troops retreated from Nsukka to Opi, leaving the town dangerously unprotected. Alarmed, James Adichie quickly tried to take his young family of his wife and two children (Ijeoma and Uchenna) home to Abba. The Biafran militia stationed at Opi instructed him to go back to the campus, presuming he was panicking. He tried again to evacuate his family but was sent back once more. It was in the third attempt that he succeeded and passed the strong-headed militia. He quickly returned alone to the University campus the following day. Now alone, he felt that Nsukka would not be taken so swiftly after all.

At about 8pm of July 9, 1967, the University Registrar, Vincent Ike, rushed in his Morris Minor car to 617 Odim street where James Adichie was staying and shouted his name severally, asking him to evacuate and leave the campus immediately. The Registrar also drove to Imoke street and shouted at one Emmanuel Ezike to evacuate too. Within thirty minutes, Adichie and his domestic hand, Melitus, rushed portable odds and ends, including his dinner for that night, into his car. He was at a lost what to pick or leave from his vast store of accumulated properties. At the end, they drove homewards towards Abba. The horde of humanity hurrying to leave Nsukka that night was touching. Some women had their children on their backs while leading others by the arm and carrying heavy loads at the same time. Others dragged goats or other young animals along with them. Indeed, it was with difficulty that Adichie maneuvered his car through the human traffic until he eased through Opi (Adichie, 2013b). A few hours later, the first artillery mortar shell landed and exploded at Nsukka. This was on Monday, July 10. The great stampede to leave Nsukka intensified. (Ike, 1989:41).

Loud sound of shelling in distant places was heard at Abba at the early stages of the war. Because of these loud reports, Adichie put his family again into his car and drove off aimlessly away from there. He drove until he got to Umuna, around Orlu area, and then began to ask about for his colleague back at the University, Emmanuel Ezike. When the man eventually saw them, he generously accepted them and fed the family as well as started making arrangements for accommodation for them. They were in his village of Umuowa at that time. Luckily enough, the family got accommodated in the man's brother's place.

The University of Nigeria had moved from Enugu (when it fell on October 4, 1967) to Umuahia (which was the capital of Biafra at the time). The University remained at Government College, Umuahia from October 1967 until the fall of Umuahia in April 1969. Some offices were at Umudike, a short distance away. The University later moved to Aboh-Mbaise and then to Emekuku Community Technical Secondary School until end of war. About October 1967, after staying a while at Umuna, Adichie left his family and went to Umuahia to join other staff of the University. He sought for and got accommodation in the house of a kinsman at Umuahia. Meanwhile, many academic staff members had been deployed to various Biafran Directorates to help in the war efforts. James Adichie was in charge of the Manpower Directorate. The main work of the Directorate was to collate people's names and where they were working before the war in order to build up a manpower database for the new Biafra. Throughout his stay at Umuahia, he experienced the heavy strafing and bombings from Nigerian war planes. Many people were killed during these air raids. Adichie was not using his car to go to work, because the war planes targeted moving vehicles quite often. The car was hidden under a camouflage of leaves to escape notice. The problem of feeding was partly solved by the relief material gotten from organizations such as CARITAS. When Umuahia fell in April 1969, James had to flee with other people. He always had made-in-Biafra petrol in his car, ready for evacuation. Incidentally, his host who had a big motorbike, refused to move. James Adichie had to drag him into his car and out of Umuahia. They drove to Umuna where the Adichie family was staying. This kinsman stayed for only two nights and trekked defiantly to Abba. He was to die some months later.

At Umuna, James made bomb shelter just like everyone else to withstand the constant bombings from the Nigerian war planes. It was very difficult getting money from the banks because no public institutions were really visible and had a direct address. They were hidden in different places in Biafra. It was at this point towards the end of war that James Adichie was informed that his father had died. News of the death of his father caused in him the greatest shock he ever got during the war. He could not believe that his father could die like every other person. During the early stages of the war, his father had refused to leave Abba. He had said he would at least kill one Nigerian soldier before they would gun him down. When the situation got worse and Nigerian soldiers were advancing into Abba and surrounding towns, neighbours had to almost drag the man away from his house before he agreed to join them in leaving Abba. They had first gone to Umunya and then to other places before they settled at Nsugbe in a refugee camp. There was no communication between him and his children, including James. There was a demarcation cutting through the Biafran country, running roughly along the long Onitsha-Enugu route. One side of the demarcation which was occupied already by Nigerian troops was called "Biafra 1",, the left side of the demarcation spreading across the rest of the Biafra country in which Biafran soldiers occupied was called "Biafra 2". While James' father was in Biafra 1, he was in Biafra 2. It was difficult and dangerous to cross over from one sector to the other. But when James heard that his father had died, he made desperate efforts to cross over to the other sector. The Biafran soldiers at the trenches along the boundary were not keen on letting him pass through. He pleaded but they were firm in their refusal. He, therefore, was not able to see the remains of his father. The war was almost coming to an end by this time. When it eventually did on January 14, 1970 which was the day that General Philip Efiong officially made a formal declaration of surrender, James Adichie and his family began to drive back to Abba. There were Nigerian soldiers everywhere and some of them were harassing the returning civilians, sometimes beating them up or even killing them. James and his family had to go through very embarrassing experiences during this time. Top Biafran government officials were being arrested so people of that cadre were camouflaging themselves in that they were returning in rags rather than in neat clothing. So the absence of the clout of status facilitated easier intimidation by the mostly semi-illiterate Nigerian soldiers. Adichie observed that the fairly educated officers were mostly Yoruba while the largely uneducated rank and file was mostly of northern origin. The latter were rough in their handling of the returning refugees. At a time, some army men stopped James Adichie and others as they were moving towards Abba and ordered them to begin to remove a pile of cement blocks which blocked off a road. James quietly obeyed the order as others did. He had hidden his car some distance away. His family, including his house help Melitus, was in the car. Years later, James Adichie observed that without the devotion of Miletus, one or more of his children would have died in the rough circumstances of the time. After executing the "order" from the soldiers, James returned to where he had packed his car and saw that it was gone. He was alarmed. He came back to the officers and told them that his car and his family were nowhere to be found. Probably because of the way he laid his complaint firmly and passionately, the officers promised to get his car back. They searched around and saw it with the rank and file soldiers. By this time, these soldiers had beaten up a member of the Adichie's family who was in the car. James swallowed the pains and moved on with his family. There were other incidences on the way to Abba, including when a rough soldier wanted to sandwich himself into the well-packed car as his own idea of hitch-hiking. James, who had by now gotten fed up with the attitude of these soldiers, firmly insisted that the ruffian got down from the car and that he was ready to be killed if the soldier stuck to his guns. James' wife pleaded with her husband to calm down. She was not ready to be a widow, not now that the war had ended. Fortunately, the soldier yielded and left the car.

Upon coming home to Abba, the Adichie family had to start from scratch. James Adichie's mother was sick and it was difficult feeding at this time. Help was to come from a friend who gave the family some money which sustained them for a considerable while.

Some valuables that were brought to the house of the Adichies by their neighbours for safekeeping at the beginning of the war had all gone with wartime looting. Some of the valuables included an elephant tusk. Unfortunately, the owner of this elephant tusk and other people who had kept things at the Adichies strangely suspected the family of stealing those valuables! This false accusation raged on for many years after the war and had to peter out with the passage of age and time.

James Adichie visited the refugee camp where his father was buried in a mass grave at Nsugbe. Stoically, Adichie quietly scooped up sand from the grave and had it preserved in a polythene bag. On returning home, he kept the memento behind his father's picture in fond and deep respect of the man who had made sure he got educated.

Adichie had to remain for some time at home before he reported at the University of Nigeria campus to resume his post as lecturer. Amidst the wreckage caused by the war, including the stark reality of having lost very valuable materials such as his PhD academic gown to wartime looting, James settled down stoically. He quietly resolved to move ahead with life, determined to excel in his chosen area of endeavour. It is instructive that not long afterwards, he and his colleagues were able to achieve the hiving off of the Statistics Department from the Department of Mathematics, Statistics and Astronomy of the University.

CHAPTER FOUR: CAREER PROGRESSION AND ADMINISTRATIVE ACHIEVEMENTS

In the University, by dint of hard work, Adichie rose quickly to senior Lecturer in 1972, Reader in 1974 and Professor of Statistics in 1976. As Professor, James moved his family to a large bungalow in Mbanefoh Street within the University campus. He produced the first M.Sc. graduate of the University of Nigeria and interestingly in Statistics in 1971 (Chief Christian Nicholas Onuoha) and another student in 1973. The quality of his research output was such that it was easy to earn regular space in such coveted and world renowned Journals as the *Annals of Mathematical statistics, Communications in Statistics* and others. He relentlessly pushed beyond the boundaries of knowledge in the area of Non-parametric Statistics. His fame spread across continents as his publications attracted international acclaim and referrals. He gave lectures and seminars in non-parametric statistics to audiences in such top institutions as the Universities of Aberystwyth, Birmingham, Sheffield, Glasgow, Cambridge and the Imperial College, London. He was invited twice to deliver lead papers in the International Conference on the Teaching of Statistics (ICOTS) in Sheffield, UK and British Columbia. He was External Examiner in Mathematics and Statistics to numerous universities (Adichie, 2013d). His supervisory and research duties included reviewership of such very high impact factor

Journals as *Annals of Mathematical Statistics, Annals of Statistics, National Science Foundation, Journal of American Statistical Association* and *Journal of the Royal Statistical Society.* Prof Adichie has had such profound effect on the discipline and profession of statistics. His footprints and signatures are ubiquitous in the world of Statistics. Generations of students who went through him testify to how their lives and academic fortunes were transformed by his wisdom, insight and fatherly encouragement. His academic contemporaries have shown by their invitations to him to deliver lectures and to attend conferences that you cannot move far in non-parametric statistics without getting his opinion on the journey so far. A man of peace, with a brain loaded with matters of statistics and matters of life and living, he picks his slow measured steps in the manner of one afraid to step on an ant. He is a calm and confident intellectual giant, a calm operator whose ambition is to get results. He is a man whose name on academic papers confers a mark of high quality.

One of the biographers, Prof. Peter I. Uche, came in contact with Prof. J.N. Adichie in 1967. This was when, as a result of the Nigerian crisis then. Prof. Uche and many other Eastern Nigerians had fled for their dear lives from the Universities outside the East. He landed in the then Department of Mathematics, Statistics and Astronomy. Prof. Uche found a welcoming Department with a vibrant programme in Statistics. The part played by Prof. Adichie in establishing, husbanding and developing the Department has been stressed earlier. It is of note that he designed elective statistics courses for other departments in the University of Nigeria. That the Department of Statistics is now one of the foremost if not the foremost Department of Statistics in the Nigerian University system is due to him. He dug the foundation and set the tone for good inter-personal relationship and for a positive and enduring attitude to work that has subsisted till today.

Today the Department has strong and highly sought after Undergraduate and Postgraduate programmes. Prof Adichie streamlined the procedure for the presentation of Postgraduate Seminars. A casual examination of the Statistics programmes of many universities will leave no one in doubt as to the impact that the Department of Statistics, University of Nigeria has had on the Statistics programme of the Nigerian University system. Graduates of the Department have made great impact in Universities across the globe. The Department is a source of academic manpower supply to many universities in the country. All these are due to the foundation laid by and the presence of Professor James N. Adichie.

Apart from the training of generations of university students, Professor J.N. Adichie has in general been the key architect of statistical education in Nigeria. When the Federal Government decided that University students should be introduced to the essentials of statistics, a Committee was set up by the National Universities Commission not only to work out modalities for achieving this but also to produce the relevant syllabus. Experts were assembled to advice on course contents. Our distinguished octogenarian was an instant choice as a member. The Committee came up with a general statistics programme for use within the General Studies Programme in all Nigerian Universities.

At this time, before the Nigeria-Biafra war, when Professor Adichie was playing his pioneering role, statistics as a discipline had the misfortune of being misunderstood by many. For some it was all about the census, for others it was only about collecting figures. Not many were aware of the depth of scientific rigour involved in the study and use of statistics. Professor Adichie was a worthy ambassador of and the voice of Statistics.

Sometime before the Nigeria – Biafra war, WAEC, under the Chairmanship of Prof. Chukwuemeka Vincent Ike, set up a Committee to consider the introduction of Statistics as a separate course in its examinations. Professor J.N. Adichie was Chairman of this Committee. The recommendations of the Committee were accepted and duly implemented by the Council. So Statistics became a subject studied on its own in Secondary Schools. Prof. Adichie became the pioneer examiner in O-Level Statistics, setting and, for many years, marking W.A.E.C. Statistics all alone. Later when the number of candidates increased, more examiners were added. Although for inexplicable reasons, this worthy innovation, the introduction of Statistics as a separate subject, was killed a few years later, credit must continue to go to Professor J.N. Adichie and his team for the increased visibility given to the subject of Statistics.

Prof. James Ezeilo took over from the Indian, Professor P.C. Chaudhuri, as Head of the Department of Mathematics, Statistics and Astronomy. He later became the acting Vice Chancellor of the University from November 1970 to March 1971. It was during this period that Professor James Adichie became the acting Head of the Department of Mathematics and Statistics. His achievements as acting Head of Department of Mathematics and Statistics in the 1970 – 1971 session include, as aforementioned, consolidating the pioneering of the teaching of Statistics in the University and introducing more and more statistics courses into the Curriculum in preparation for a complete hive of Statistics from the Department of Mathematics, Statistics and Astronomy. Students began to graduate in Statistics. One of the biographers, Prof. Peter Ikechukwu Uche had the privilege of being lectured and nurtured by Prof. James Adichie. He graduated in 1971 with a BSc. (First Class Honours) in Statistics. There was also another outstanding graduate, Cyprian Anaene Oyeka. Also in 1971, the postgraduate student, Christian Nicholas Onuoha, earned a postgraduate degree in Statistics. Indeed, there was an unprecedented influx of students who wanted to study Statistics, especially because it was new, thanks to Onuoha's achievement as first Masters Graduate of the University. To students also, Statistics was a new and exciting field of study, or so it seemed to them. Soon, getting a degree in Statistics or Mathematics became optional as approved by Senate for the Department of Mathematics, Statistics and Astronomy. Fortunately, a separate Department of Statistics was established in 1973. Adichie became Head of Department of Statistics from 1973 to 1979 and again from 1985 to 1989. As Head, he began to encourage and consolidate his facilitation of the easy study leave of already employed graduate students for postgraduate programmes in Statistics under the Junior Fellowship Scheme. Peter Uche was to go to the University of Sheffield in the United Kingdom under this arrangement, obtaining MSc and PhD degrees in 1973 and 1975 respectively. Other students who began to take Statistics seriously as a field of study and who were employed by the University of Nigeria because of the nurturing of Adichie included Christian Chiechefulam Agunwamba (graduated 1972) etc.

Adichie was appointed the Dean, Faculty of Physical Sciences in the 1979/80 session. During his tenure, his former student, Christian Onuoha, was the Head of Department of Statistics. Adichie used his position as Dean to influence more concretization of the constructive interests of the Department of Statistics. He also oversaw and ensured the smooth running of the other departments in Faculty of the Physical Sciences at the time. At this time, the other departments were Chemistry, Geology, Mathematics and Physics.

Adichie was suddenly called up to the position of Deputy Vice-Chancellor, Nsukka Campus for four years from 1 August 1980 to 31 July 1984. As DVC responsible for deputizing for the Vice Chancellor in both administrative and academic matters that concerns the University of Nigeria, he played very important mediatory role during those crisis-filled days of the University. His acute intelligence ensured that there were some checks in the momentum of the tumult that was being stirred because of the circumstances and makeup of the different high-ranking personalities who peopled the University system at the time. The Vice Chancellor at this time was Professor Frank Nwachukwu Ndili.

Professor Adichie went on Sabbatical as Visiting Professor to San Diego State University, California, in the 1984/85 session. On his return, he continued to develop the Department of Statistics in the University of Nigeria, Nsukka until his retirement.

By virtue of his generation but most importantly as a Statistician of international repute, it is not surprising that whenever and wherever Statistics was mentioned, Professor J.N. Adichie's name naturally and automatically came up. When at the behest of the Mathematical guru and visionary, Professor J.O.C. Ezeilo of blessed memory, the Federal Government of Nigeria agreed to look into the setting up of a Centre for Mathematical Sciences in the mould of the Abdus Salam International Centre of Theoretical Physics (ICTP) in Trieste, Italy, an Ad Hoc Committee was set up in 1987. Professor J.N. Adichie was a key member of this twelve-man Committee. Other members were Prof. James Ezeilo (Chairman), Prof. Alex Animalu (Secretary), Prof. R.F.A. Abiodun etc. The recommendations of this Committee led to the setting up of the National Mathematical Centre, Abuja. Statistics was one of the four Units comprising the Centre. Prof. James Ezeilo became the first Director of the National Mathematical Centre in 1989. Later, when Prof. Alex Animalu (one of the biographers) became the Director of the National Mathematical Centre in 1999, he invited Prof. James Adichie to be the Coordinator for Statistics programmes. Thus, Adichie became the first Statistics Coordinator in the Centre. He was able to organize statistics courses on assumption of duty, a feat that was not achieved before his arrival.

Writing about Professor J.N. Adichie is a joy and a privilege. Here is a man, an intellectual colossus, who has left footprints on the sands of time. Here is a man who loves what he does; getting to the root of a problem is his second nature. It is indeed a privilege for the students who have gone under his tutelage. His unapologetic attitude to hard work is infectious. His life mission is clearly to establish the teaching and learning of Statistics in Nigeria and he had little choice in the matter. His philosophy of life is the conscious and constant development of the habit of honest hard work. He urges students to moderate their lifestyles. The penchant for going to parties when one should be studying has to be minimized. Success is sure when hard work is applied. Hard work, honest hard work, is the answer.

It is fitting that a trumpet be blared from the roof tops in celebration of the monumental achievements of this teacher and researcher par excellence, a man who because of the thorough way that he addresses both work and leisure is fondly called by his traditional Ozo title, *Nwawuluaru*. He is the good shepherd who shares a sacred bond with his sheep and he is eminently worthy of all the encomiums.

Today, Prof. Adichie lives happily with his wife near the University of Nigeria at Nsukka and from time to time, their adult children come around to play the children they once were in a house full of fun.

On this special occasion of the deserved celebration of his eightieth birthday and on behalf of all whose lives were touched and shaped by Professor J.N. Adichie, we say congratulations to him and we pray that God may give him many more years of a healthy life in the midst of his family, colleagues, friends and generations of appreciative students. *AD MULTOS ANNOS!!!*

CHAPTER FOUR:
FAMILY LIFE

Among the children of the James Adichie family is his renowned novelist daughter Chimamanda Ngozi Adichie. She was born in 1977. She grew up on the University of Nigeria's Nsukka campus where her father was a statistics professor. The Adichie family was then living in 305 Margaret Cartwright Avenue, which was the former home of the novelist Chinua Achebe. At 19, Chimamanda had moved to the US where she studied communications and political science and her second novel, *Half of a Yellow Sun*, won the 2007 Orange Prize. In the Observer, Sunday 15 June, 2008 under the caption "As a child, I thought my father invincible. I also thought him remote" she gave the following lucid and graphic details about Professor James Adichie's family life (reproduced hereunder with permission):

"My father walks differently now. He is still brisk - he takes a walk most mornings, wearing sneakers and a baseball cap - but not as brisk as he used to be, and there is a tilt in his gait, a fragility: it is an old-man walk. When I first noticed this we were in our ancestral hometown, Abba, and I stood at a window watching as he walked across the compound, a small man with the darkest, loveliest umber-toned skin that has aged well; he could pass for 10 years younger than his 76 years.

The middle of his head is bald and the sparse hair surrounding it is so soft my brother Kene has difficulty cutting it with clippers. My father says that he and his sister got their mother's hair while my Uncle Mike ended up with tough hair. He has said this many times. My father repeats stories now. When I tell him that he has told a story before, he glances at me for a moment, says, 'Eziokwu, have I really?' and goes on to tell it anyway. But I still listen, still ask him to explain ornate Igbo proverbs, still imagine the grandfather I never knew who in the late 1930s sold his valuables to pay school fees for his little boy, placed the child on a bicycle every morning and determinedly rode miles to the school in Nimo because a western education was key to succeeding in the new colonial state.

That child, my father, would drop out of secondary school when his family could no longer afford the fees, would work as a sanitary inspector, take his Cambridge exams as a private candidate, study pure mathematics at Ibadan, get a doctorate at Berkeley and become Nigeria's first professor of statistics; I grew up seeing sheets of paper full of strange-looking equations on the study table. When I took mathematics problems to him, he would look at them, rub his fingers together, tell me the answer, and then struggle to find simple ways to explain it to me.

Our family myth was that he never slept: Daddy was there in his study when you woke up to pee, talking to himself, shuffling papers. As a child, I thought him invincible. I also thought him remote. My mother called our friends by their nicknames, wanted to feed everyone, and laughed a lot. My father did not pay attention to our friends, did not go to the staff club to socialise, or play tennis, or drink. He was proper and precise and reserved.

I sometimes try to remember the exact moment when I began to look at him with gratitude, and to learn from being with him that it is possible to have a kind of complete joy in the mere presence of one's father. Perhaps it was when I became old enough to see him as a funny, kind, gentle person and not just the stoic shadow in the study to whom we gave our list of Things Needed for School. He kept all of those lists. He has a steel cabinet full of the records of his six children, of the house-helps who have come and gone over the years, of household expenses.

Now he writes down things and forgets where he wrote them. 'I look for my glasses when I have them on,' he says, and shakes his head, laughing at himself. His humour was always dry. Now it is more playful. Recently he and I were in a Connecticut store when a man brushed past us, and rudely said: 'Excuse me!' A stocky and unattractive man. After he walked past, my father said in Igbo, his face expressionless: 'What a tall handsome man.'

My father's stories digress now. He tells them with humour and nostalgia, lapsing into songs from his childhood, saying he recently ran into so-and-so with whom he had wrestled as a child and so-and-so no longer had any teeth. Most of his contemporaries did not get the education he did, and I still hear stories of how people in our hometown would insist that any formal documentation from the government be kept until my father came home so he would explain it to them. They call him by his title Odeluora: He Who Writes for the

Community. As we, his children, sometimes do. At my graduation, my father gave a long, story-filled toast, raising the bottle of champagne and saluting his dead father, asking specific blessings for each of us, and at the end we all called out, 'Odeluora!' (We 'hailed him', in Nigeria-speak).

My father has been devoutly Roman Catholic all his life. On the living-room wall of the flat he shares with my mother there is a photo of him in the formal regalia of the Knights of St Mulumba: he is holding a sword, wearing an elaborate green cape and a yacht-like hat [See picture Gallery]. My brother Okey says he looks like a superhero just about to fly off. Whenever my father travels out of Nigeria, we tease him about not taking his knightly sword, because of possible problems with airport security. My mother complains that when he wakes up at five to go to mass he turns on the light too brightly and, worse, sings as he gets ready.

He insists he has no need for new clothes. 'This shirt is very good. I bought it in London in 1975,' he'll say with that peculiar Nigerian assumption that anything purchased abroad is superior. My fashionable sister Uche will say, 'The collar is frayed, Daddy.' 'It's perfectly fine,' he will retort. But we buy him new clothes anyway and in his closet there is a pile of unworn shirts.

I came, as an adult, to deeply admire the contented simplicity in my father's nature. My sister Ijeoma says he is a man who stretches whatever soup he has to make it sufficient for his pounded yam. Or in my brother Chuk's words, my father is a man who 'doesn't have trouble'.

Some people wear their unimpressionable nature like a shiny medal but he doesn't; it simply does not occur to him to think of the Joneses. In a country, Nigeria, where material wealth is often overemphasized, he has minimal interest in who has what. Perhaps it is why he takes great pleasure in little things: in watching the antics of a goat tied to a tree, in reading a map. A show on Animal Planet leaves him laughing with absolute delight, and when he laughs, sitting down, he sometimes raises one leg from the floor. Last Christmas most of my family gathered in Abba. Five of my father's six children. Four of his six grandchildren. Watching us, my father said: 'Ndi be Adichie.' The Adichie family. And there was wonder in his voice".

Professor James Nwoye Adichie also gives us a glimpse into the way he brought up his children in this interview he granted to the Education Review section of *The Sun* newspapers of August 31, 2012 entitled, 'How I trained Chimamanda and her siblings to speak and write Igbo'. Excerpts:

"When I was in United States, I was teaching my children Igbo language. I am a traditional Igbo man. Because of that I would not like my children not to understand or speak our language. You can speak French. You can speak Spanish. You can speak American English. You can speak whatever foreign language you like, but you must understand that you are an Igbo before you came in contact with these other languages.

That was why my wife and I decided when our first child was two years old and she had started talking, that we would not use English, but Igbo to speak to her whenever she came back from school. 'Jee ka i wetara m afere ebee ni' (Go get me that plate for me over there), we would say. You know, simple words, phrases or commands like that. 'Go and do this.' 'Go and do that', all in Igbo and she would listen and obey.

And it helped her. By the time we got home, she was able to understand when spoken to in Igbo and she would also reply in Igbo. People were impressed. "Today, all my children, including Chimamanda, can speak and write Igbo language very well because my wife and I made sure we brought them up in Igbo while they were with us in the home. I blame parents who don't teach their children our language.

And I want to appeal to parents who have their home outside Igboland to try and make their children understand and speak our language. It is very, very important. That doesn't mean that if they are in the U.S. or UK, for instance, their children will not be able to speak good English when they go to school. It is not true. At least, I have proved that. "Within their home, parents should insist on their children speaking Igbo because it will help them to keep their identity while trying to reach out to the outside world. We are all responsible for the poor state of Igbo language today and I don't know what we can do to reverse the hand of the clock. Most times, when people go home for an occasion or something like that, you find them speaking English.

That kind of thing should not be encouraged. In Abba, my hometown, I am known as an old conservative person. In every meeting we have, I always insist that we must speak Igbo because it is the language of our people but sometimes not everybody is happy with that, especially the young ones, because they are not fluent in Igbo. You would see some of them complaining that they cannot speak Igbo.

But we shouldn't let our language die because of that. And, we shouldn't be ashamed to speak our language. That doesn't make us less than anything we are as intellectuals. It will be a great tragedy if we allow our language to die off. And, if that happens, that means we have no more identity. I know there are some organizations that are doing everything possible to revive the Igbo language. I think they should be encouraged."

Other glimpses into the Adichie family life can be gotten from the tributes sent by the family in Chapter Seven.

CHAPTER FIVE: SELECTED ARTICLES OF PROFESSOR JAMES N. ADICHIE

ASYMPTOTIC EFFICIENCY OF A CLASS OF NON-PARAMETRIC TESTS FOR REGRESSION PARAMETERS[1]

By J. N. Adichie

University of Nigeria, Nsukka, and University of California, Berkeley

0. Introduction and summary. For testing hypotheses about α and β in the linear regression model $Y_j = \alpha + \beta x_j + Z_j$, Brown and Mood [18] have proposed distribution-free tests, based on their median estimates. Daniels [6] has also given a distribution-free test for the hypothesis that the regression parameters have specified values. This latter test is an improvement on the Brown and Mood median procedure, although both are based on the signs of the observations. Recently Hájek [10] constructed rank tests, which are asymptotically most powerful, for testing the hypothesis that $\beta = 0$, while α is regarded as a nuisance parameter.

In this paper, a class of rank score tests for the hypothesis $H: \alpha = \beta = 0$, is proposed in Section 2. This class includes as special cases, the Wilcoxon and the normal scores type of tests. In Sections 3 and 4 the limiting distribution of the test statistics is shown to be central χ^2, under H, and non-central χ^2, under a sequence of alternatives tending to the hypothesis at a suitable rate. In Section 5, the Pitman efficiency of the proposed tests relative to the classical F-test, is proved to be the same as the efficiency of the corresponding rank score tests relative to the t-test in the two sample problem.

1. Assumptions and notations. Let $(Y_{n1}, \cdots, Y_{nn})$ be a sequence of random vectors, where Y_{nj}, $j = 1, \cdots, n$, are independent with distributions

$$P_{\alpha\beta}(Y_{nj} \leqq y) = F(y - \alpha - \beta x_{nj}) \tag{1.1}$$

where $P_{\alpha\beta}$ denotes that the probability is being computed for the parameter values α and β.

The x_{nj} are known constants depending on n; and we shall suppress this dependence in our notation, whenever this causes no confusion. The problem here is to construct rank score tests for the hypothesis $H: \alpha = \beta = 0$. The form of F is not known but we shall assume only that $F \varepsilon \mathfrak{F}$, where

$$\begin{aligned} \mathfrak{F} = \{&\text{absolutely continuous } F: \\ &\text{(i) } F'(y) = f(y) \text{ is absolutely continuous,} \\ &\text{(ii) } \textstyle\int_{-\infty}^{\infty} (f'(y)/f(y))^2 f(y)\, dy \text{ is finite,} \\ &\text{(iii) } f(-y) = f(y)\}. \end{aligned} \tag{1.2}$$

Received 27 July 1966; revised 30 January 1967.

[1] This research was supported in part by the Agency for International Development under contract MSU AIDc-1398, and in part by the National Science Foundation, Grant GP-5059.

We shall also assume that the constants x_j, $j = 1, \cdots, n$, satisfy the following conditions:

$$(1.3) \qquad \lim [\{\max_j (x_j - \bar{x}_n)^2\}/\{\textstyle\sum_j (x_j - \bar{x}_n)^2\}] = 0,$$

$$(1.4) \qquad \lim [n^{-1} \textstyle\sum_j (x_j - \bar{x}_n)^2] < \infty, \qquad |\lim \bar{x}_n| < \infty,$$

$$(1.5) \qquad \lim n^{-1} \textstyle\sum_j (x_j - \bar{x}_n)^2 > 0,$$

where $\bar{x}_n = n^{-1} \sum_j x_j$, and the summation goes from 1 to n.

All limits in this paper unless otherwise stated are taken as $n \to \infty$. We shall write $\mathfrak{L}(X_n \mid P) \to N(a, b^2)$ to denote that the distribution law of $(X_n - a)/b$ tends to the standard normal distribution under P. The following class of functions shall be used in the sequel.

$$(1.6) \qquad \psi(u) = -[g'(G^{-1}(\tfrac{1}{2}u + \tfrac{1}{2}))/g(G^{-1}(\tfrac{1}{2}u + \tfrac{1}{2}))], \qquad 0 < u < 1,$$

where G^{-1} is the inverse of G, and G is any known distribution function belonging to the class $\mathfrak{F}$. The (1.6)-function that corresponds to F is

$$(1.7) \qquad \varphi(u) = -[f'(F^{-1}(\tfrac{1}{2}u + \tfrac{1}{2}))/f(F^{-1}(\tfrac{1}{2}u + \tfrac{1}{2}))], \qquad 0 < u < 1.$$

Observe that unlike $\psi(u)$ of (1.6), $\varphi(u)$ is not known since it is defined through the unknown F.

2. A class of test statistics. Let R_j be the rank of $|Y_j|$ in the sequence of absolute values $|Y_1|, \cdots, |Y_n|$ of the n observations. Consider a pair of statistics T_1 and T_2 defined by

$$(2.1) \qquad T_1(Y) = n^{-1} \textstyle\sum_j \psi_n(R_j/n + 1) \operatorname{Sign} Y_j,$$

$$(2.2) \qquad T_2(Y) = n^{-1} \textstyle\sum_j x_j \psi_n(R_j/n + 1) \operatorname{Sign} Y_j,$$

where

$$(2.3) \qquad \psi_n(u) = \psi(j/n + 1), \qquad (j - 1)/n < u \leqq j/n,$$

and

$$(2.4) \qquad \lim \textstyle\int_0^1 [\psi_n(u) - \psi(u)]^2 \, du = 0$$

by [9]. Let a symmetric 2×2 matrix $\|\gamma_{kl}\|_n$ be given by

$$(2.5) \qquad \gamma_{11} = \textstyle\int_0^1 \psi^2(u)\, du; \qquad \gamma_{22,n} = n^{-1} \sum_j x_j^2 \int_0^1 \psi^2(u)\, du;$$

$$\gamma_{21,n} = n^{-1} \textstyle\sum_j x_j \int_0^1 \psi^2(u)\, du.$$

Define

$$(2.6) \qquad M(\psi) = n(T_1, T_2)\|\gamma_{kl}\|_n^{-1} (T_1, T_2)'$$

where $(\mathbf{V})'$ denotes the transpose of $(\mathbf{V})$, and $\|\gamma_{kl}\|_n^{-1}$ is the inverse of $\|\gamma_{kl}\|_n$. We propose $M(\psi)$ as the class of test statistics for the hypothesis $H: \alpha = \beta = 0$.

Observe that M is well defined since both $\|\gamma_{kl}\|_n^{-1}$ and its limit as $n \to \infty$, exist by (1.5).

To every $G \varepsilon \mathfrak{F}$, corresponds one test statistic M. In particular, if G is the logistic distribution function $G(y) = \{1 + \exp(-y)\}^{-1}$, it can easily be checked that $\psi(u) = u$. The corresponding test statistic M, defined through $T_1(Y) = n^{-1} \sum_j (R_j/n + 1)$ Sign Y_j and $T_2(Y) = n^{-1} \sum_j x_j(R_j/n + 1)$ Sign Y_j is said to be of the Wilcoxon type. If G is chosen to be the normal distribution function Φ, then $\psi(u) = \Phi^{-1}(\frac{1}{2}u + \frac{1}{2})$ and the corresponding M-statistic is said to be of the Van der Waerden (normal scores) type. On taking G to be the double exponential distribution function, $\psi(u)$ reduces to unity, and the corresponding M-statistic defined through $T_1(Y) = n^{-1} \sum_j$ Sign Y_j, and $T_2(Y) = n^{-1} \sum_j x_j$ Sign Y_j is said to be of the sign type. We remark that the components T_1 and T_2 of M, are familiar for we recognize T_1 as being equivalent to the usual rank score statistic for the one sample problem [8], while T_2 is similar to Hájek's statistic for the test of symmetry [10].

3. Limiting distribution of M under the hypothesis. We note that under H, the joint distribution of T_1 and T_2 is independent of F, but depends only on the function ψ and hence on G, through which ψ is defined. The following theorem gives the limiting null distribution of M.

THEOREM 3.1. *Under the assumptions of Section 2,*

$$\lim P_0(M \leqq y) = P(\chi_2^2 \leqq y)$$

where χ_2^2 denotes the central chi-square random variable, with 2 degrees of freedom, and P_0 denotes that the probability is computed under $H: \alpha = \beta = 0$.

PROOF. It suffices to prove that $\mathfrak{L}(n^{\frac{1}{2}}(T_1, T_2) | P_0)$ tends to the bivariate normal distribution with covariance matrix $\|\gamma_{kl}\| = \lim \|\gamma_{kl}\|_n$. The idea of the proof is as in [10] to replace T_i, $i = 1, 2$, by sums of independent random variables and apply the central limit theorem.

Now introduce two statistics,

$$S_1^{(0)} = n^{-1} \sum_j \psi_n(F^*(|Y_j|)) \text{ Sign } Y_j \tag{3.1}$$

and

$$S_2^{(0)} = n^{-1} \sum_j x_j \psi_n(F^*(|Y_j|)) \text{ Sign } Y_j \tag{3.2}$$

where F^* is the distribution function of $|Y_j|$, i.e. $P_0\{|Y_j| \leqq y\} = F^*(y) = 2F(y) - 1$ for $y > 0$. Because the vectors $(R_1, \cdots, R_n)$, $(|Y_1|, \cdots, |Y_n|)$ and (Sign $Y_1, \cdots,$ Sign Y_n) are mutually independent, and $E_0(\text{sign } Y_j) = 0$ for all j, we have

$$\begin{aligned} E_0\{n^{\frac{1}{2}}(T_2 - S_2^{(0)})\}^2 &= \text{Var}_0 \{n^{\frac{1}{2}}(T_2 - S_2^{(0)})\} \\ &= n^{-1} \sum_j x_j^2 E_0[\psi_n(R_j/n + 1) - \psi_n(U_j)]^2 \end{aligned}$$

where $U_j = F^*(|Y_j|)$ are independent random variables uniformly distributed on $(0, 1)$. Clearly

$$E_0[\psi_n(R_j/n + 1) - \psi_n(U_j)]^2 = E_0[\psi_n(R_1/n + 1) - \psi_n(U_1)]^2$$

for every $j = 1, \cdots, n$. Using Lemma 2.1 of [9], and (1.4), it is seen that

(3.3) $$n^{\frac{1}{2}}(T_i - S_i^{(0)}) \to 0 \quad \text{in} \quad P_0\text{-probability}, \qquad i = 1, 2.$$

Let

(3.4) $$S_1 = n^{-\frac{1}{2}} \sum_j \psi(U_j) \text{ Sign } Y_j$$

and

(3.5) $$S_2 = n^{-1} \sum_j x_j \psi(U_j) \text{ Sign } Y_j,$$

where $U_j = F^*(|Y_j|)$. Due to the independence of $|Y_j|$ and Sign Y_j, we have

$$\begin{aligned} E_0[n^{\frac{1}{2}}(S_2^{(0)} - S_2)]^2 &= \text{Var}_0 \{n^{\frac{1}{2}}(S_2^{(0)} - S_2)\} \\ &= n^{-1} \sum_j x_j^2 E_0[\psi_n(F^*(|Y_j|)) - \psi(F^*(|Y_j|))]^2 \\ &= n^{-\frac{1}{2}} \sum_j x_j^2 \int_0^1 [\psi_n(u) - \dot{\psi}(u)]^2 \, du \to 0. \end{aligned}$$

Hence

(3.6) $$n^{\frac{1}{2}}(S_i^{(0)} - S_i) \to 0 \quad \text{in} \quad P_0\text{-probability}, \qquad i = 1, 2.$$

On combining (3.3) and (3.6), we obtain that for $i = 1, 2$,

(3.7) $$n^{\frac{1}{2}}(T_i - S_i) \to 0 \quad \text{in} \quad P_0\text{-probability}.$$

Because the $\psi(U_j), j = 1, \cdots, n$, are independent identically distributed random variables, which are also independent of sign Y_j, the central limit theorem gives immediately

(3.8) $$\mathfrak{L}(n^{\frac{1}{2}}T_1 \mid P_0) \to N(0, \gamma_{11}) = N(0, \gamma_1^2).$$

On the other hand, it is clear that the general central limit theorem (Loève [17], Theorem B, p. 280) applies to $n^{\frac{1}{2}}S_2$, and on account of (3.7), we also obtain that,

(3.9) $$\mathfrak{L}(n^{\frac{1}{2}}T_2 \mid P_0) \to N(0, \gamma_{22}) = N(0, \gamma_2^2)$$

where $\gamma_{22} = \lim \gamma_{22,n}$ defined in (2.5). To prove the joint asymptotic normality of $n^{\frac{1}{2}}T_1$ and $n^{\frac{1}{2}}T_2$, it is sufficient, because of (3.7) and a well known theorem(Cramér [4], p, 299), to establish the joint asymptotic normality of $n^{\frac{1}{2}}S_1$ and $n^{\frac{1}{2}}S_2$.

But for any arbitrary λ_1 and λ_2, $n^{\frac{1}{2}}(\lambda_1 S_1 + \lambda_2 S_2) = n^{-\frac{1}{2}} \sum_j x_j^* \psi(U_j)$ Sign Y_j where x_j^* satisfy conditions (1.3) and (1.4). It follows that

$$\mathfrak{L}(n^{\frac{1}{2}}(\lambda_1 T_1 + \lambda_2 T_2) \mid P_0)$$

tends to a normal distribution, and hence that $\mathfrak{L}(n^{\frac{1}{2}}(T_1, T_2) \mid P_0)$ tends to the bivariate normal distribution with zero means, and covariance matrix $\|\gamma_{kl}\|$. The assertion of the theorem follows by the usual transformation, see for example Sverdrup [21].

As a direct consequence of Theorem 3.1, it follows that the critical function

$$\begin{aligned} \varphi(M) &= 1 \quad \text{if} \quad M > \chi^2_{2,\epsilon} \\ &= 0 \quad \text{otherwise} \end{aligned}$$

where $\chi^2_{2,\epsilon}$ is the $100(1 - \epsilon)\%$ point of the χ^2 distribution with 2 degrees of freedom, provides an asymptotic level ϵ test of H.

4. Limiting distribution of M under near alternatives. In order to determine the efficiency of the class $M(\psi)$ of test statistics, it is necessary to find its distribution under a sequence of alternatives tending to the hypothesis, at a suitable rate. In this section we discuss the distribution of M for alternatives tending to H at the rate of $n^{-\frac{1}{2}}$; and for this, we shall follow the method based on Le Cam's contiguity lemma [10] and [15]. First we give the set-up under which the contiguity principle is applicable.

Let $P_n = \prod_{j=1}^{n} P_j$ be the distributions of $(Y_1, \cdots, Y_n)$ under a sequence K_n of alternatives defined by

$$(4.1) \qquad K_n : \alpha_n = an^{-\frac{1}{2}}; \qquad \beta_n = bn^{-\frac{1}{2}}$$

and let

$$(4.2) \qquad r_j = p_j(Y_j)/p_0(Y_j) \qquad \text{for} \quad p_0(y) > 0$$

where $p_j, j = 1, \cdots, n$, are densities corresponding to P_j, and p_0 corresponds to the distribution P_0, under the hypothesis.

Define

$$(4.3) \qquad W_n = 2 \textstyle\sum_j (r_j^{\frac{1}{2}} - 1).$$

With the above notation, we shall prove the following:

LEMMA 4.1. *If* (1.2), (1.3) *and* (1.4) *hold, and P_n are the distributions under K_n given in* (4.1), *then P_n are contiguous to P_0.*

PROOF. The lemma will be proved if we show that

(i) $\lim \max_j P_0(|r_j - 1| > \epsilon) = 0$ for every $\epsilon > 0$, and

(ii) $\mathcal{L}(W_n \mid P_0) \to N(-\frac{1}{4}\sigma^2, \sigma^2)$.

For (i), write $r_j = f(Y_j - h_j)/f(Y_j)$ where $h_j = n^{-\frac{1}{2}}(a + bx_j)$ and we may assume $h_j \neq 0$. Again the dependence on n of h_j is suppressed. Then

$$\max_j P_0(|r_j - 1| > \epsilon) \leqq \max_j \epsilon^{-1} E_0 |r_j - 1|$$
$$= \max_j \epsilon^{-1} |h_j| \int_{\infty}^{\infty} |h_j^{-1}\{f(y - h_j) - f(y)\}|\, dy.$$

Now

$$|h_j^{-1}\{f(y - h_j) - f(y)\}| \leqq |h_j^{-1}| \int_{y-h_j}^{y} |f'(x)|\, dx,$$

and

$$\int_{-\infty}^{\infty} |h_j^{-1}\{f(y - h_j) - f(y)\}|\, dy \leqq \int_{-\infty}^{\infty} |f'(y)|\, dy \quad \text{for all} \quad j = 1, \cdots, n.$$

Hence we have that

$$\max_j P_0\{|r_j - 1| > \epsilon\} \leqq \max_j \epsilon^{-1} |h_j| \int_{-\infty}^{\infty} |f'(y)|\, dy \to 0.$$

To prove (ii), define

$$(4.4) \qquad S_n^* = n^{-1} \textstyle\sum_j (a + bx_j) f'(Y_j)/f(Y_j),$$

where $f'(x) = d/dxf(x)$, and write W_n in the form

$$(4.5) \qquad W_n = 2 \sum_j [\{s(Y_j - h_j)/s(Y_j)\} - 1],$$

where $s(x) = f^{\frac{1}{2}}(x)$. It can be seen that

$$(4.6) \qquad E_0 W_n \sim -\sigma_n^2/4$$

and that

$$(4.7) \qquad \text{Var}_0\,(n^{\frac{1}{2}} S_n^*) = \sigma_n^2$$

where $\sigma_n^2 = \sum_j h_j^2 \int_{-\infty}^{\infty} (f'(y)/f(y))^2 f(y)\, dy = \sum_j h_j^2 \int_0^1 \varphi^2(u)\, du$. Furthermore,

$$(4.8) \quad E_0(W_n - E_0 W_n - n^{\frac{1}{2}} S_n^*)$$
$$\leqq 4 \sum_j h_j^2 \int_{-\infty}^{\infty} [h_j^{-1}\{s(y - h_j) - s(y)\} - s'(y)]^{12}\, dy$$

and the right hand side of (4.8) tends to zero by (1.4) and Lemma 4.3 of [10]. The limiting distribution of $n^{\frac{1}{2}} S_n^*$ is of course normal with zero mean and variance $\sigma^2 = \lim \sigma_n^2$. It follows from (4.6) and (4.8) that $\mathcal{L}(W_n \mid P_0) \to N(-\frac{1}{4}\sigma^2, \sigma^2)$, and the proof of the lemma is therefore complete.

We shall now apply the contiguity principle to obtain the limit distribution of (T_1, T_2) under the sequence K_n of alternatives. The main result of this section is the following:

THEOREM 4.1. *Under the assumptions of Lemma* 4.1, $\mathcal{L}(n^{\frac{1}{2}}(T_1, T_2) \mid P_n)$ *tends to the bivariate normal distribution with mean vector* (μ_1, μ_2) *and covariance matrix* $\|\gamma_{kl}\|$, *where the means are defined by:*

$$(4.9) \qquad \mu_1 = \lim n^{-1} \sum_j (a + bx_j) \int_0^1 \psi(u)\varphi(u)\, du,$$
$$\mu_2 = \lim n^{-1} \sum_j x_j (a + bx_j) \int_0^1 \psi(u)\varphi(u)\, du$$

and the functions ψ *and* φ *are defined in* (1.6) and (1.7) *respectively.*

PROOF. We shall first prove that $\mathcal{L}(n^{\frac{1}{2}} T_i \mid P_n) \to N(\mu_i, \gamma_i^2)$, $i = 1, 2$, then show that (T_1, T_2) has a joint asymptotic normal distribution under K_n. By the contiguity principle the first one will follow if we prove that

(a) $\mathcal{L}(n^{\frac{1}{2}} T_i, W_n \mid P_0)$, $i = 1, 2$, tend to bivariate normal distributions with certain correlation coefficients ρ_i, and W_n is as defined in (4.3);

(b) $\mu_i = \rho_i \sigma \gamma_i$, where σ^2 is the limit of σ_n^2 defined in (4.7).

By (3.7) and (4.8) it is sufficient to consider $\mathcal{L}(n^{\frac{1}{2}}(S_i, S_n^*) \mid P_0)$. Also due to the symmetry of the density function f, we may write S_n^* of (4.4), as

$$S_n^* = n^{-1} \sum_j (a + bx_j) f^{*\prime}(|Y_j|)/f^*(|Y_j|) \text{ Sign } Y_j$$
$$= n^{-1} \sum_j (a + bx_j)\varphi(U_j) \text{ Sign } Y_j$$

where f^* is the density function corresponding to the distribution function F^* of $|Y_j|$. Now

$$n(S_2, S_n^*) = [\sum_j x_j \psi(U_j), \sum_j (a + bx_j)\varphi(U_j)] \text{ Sign } Y_j,$$

so that

$$\text{Cov}_0\,[n^{\frac{1}{2}}(S_2\,,\,S_n^*)] = n^{-1}\sum_j x_j(a+bx_j)\int_0^1 \psi(u)\varphi(u)\,du$$

which, by (1.4) tends to a finite limit. Furthermore it can be seen that under conditions (1.3) and (1.4) the bivariate central limit theorem (Cramér [5], p. 114, Theorem 21a) applies to $n^{\frac{1}{2}}(S_i\,,\,S_n^*)$, $i = 1, 2$, giving that $\mathcal{L}(n^{\frac{1}{2}}(S_i\,,\,S_n^*)\,|\,P_0)$ tend to the bivariate normal distributions with correlation coefficients ρ_i where

$$\rho_1 = \lim\,\{n^{-1}\sum_j (a+bx_j)\int_0^1 \psi(u)\varphi(u)\,du \cdot [n^{-1}\sum_j (a+bx_j)^2\int_0^1 \psi^2(u)\,du\int_0^1 \varphi(u)\,du]^{-\frac{1}{2}}\},$$

$$\rho_2 = \lim\,\{n^{-1}\sum_j x_j(a+bx_j)\int_0^1 \psi(u)\varphi(u)\,du \cdot [n^{-1}\sum_j (a+bx_j)^2\int_0^1 \psi^2(\text{u})\,du\int_0^1 \varphi^2(u)\,du]^{-1}\}.$$

Finally it is immediate that $\mu_i = \rho_i\sigma\gamma_i$, hence we have proved that $\mathcal{L}(n^{\frac{1}{2}}T_i\,|\,P_n) \to N(\mu_i\,,\,\gamma_i^2)$, $i = 1, 2$.

For the joint asymptotic distribution of T_1 and T_2 under K_n, note that

$$\text{(4.10)}\quad \lim \mathcal{L}(n^{\frac{1}{2}}(\lambda_1T_1+\lambda_2T_2),\,W_n\,|\,P_0) = \lim \mathcal{L}(n^{\frac{1}{2}}(\lambda_1S_1+\lambda_2S_2),\,S_n^*\,|\,P_0)$$

which by Theorem 21a of [5], is a bivariate normal. We have also shown that $\mathcal{L}(n^{\frac{1}{2}}(\lambda_1S_1+\lambda_2S_2)\,|\,P_0)$ is asymptotically normal. This fact, together with (4.10) implies that $\mathcal{L}(n^{\frac{1}{2}}(\lambda_1S_1+\lambda_2S_2)\,|\,P_n)$ is also asymptotically normal. Since λ_1 and λ_2 are arbitrary, it follows that $n^{\frac{1}{2}}(T_1\,,\,T_2)$ has a limiting bivariate normal under K_n. This completes the proof of Theorem 4.1.

We are now in the position to give the limit distribution of M, and this is stated in the following:

THEOREM 4.2. *Under the assumptions of Lemma* 4.1, $\mathcal{L}(M\,|\,P_n) \to \mathcal{L}(\chi_2^2(\Delta^2))$ *where* $\chi_2^2(\Delta^2)$ *denotes the non-central chi-square random variable with* 2 *degrees of freedom and non-centrality parameter* Δ^2 *given by*

$$\text{(4.11)}\qquad \Delta^2 = \lim\,(a^2+2ab\bar{x}_n+b^2n^{-1}\textstyle\sum_j x_j^2)(\int\psi\varphi)^2/\int\psi^2.$$

PROOF. The proof follows directly from Theorem 4.1, and Δ^2 is obtained by straightforward computation.

5. Asymptotic efficiency of M-tests. We employ a measure of relative efficiency of two test statistics due to Pitman (see Noether [19]). If under the same sequence of alternatives, the two test statistics have non-central chi square limit distributions, with the same degrees of freedom, it has been shown by Andrews [2] and Hannan [11], that their relative asymptotic efficiency is given by the ratio of their non-centrality parameters. To find the asymptotic efficiency of the M-tests relative to the classical F-test, we need therefore, to compute the non-centrality parameter of the latter.

The classical test statistic $\tilde{M}$ for H is based on a quadratic function in the least squares estimates $\tilde{\alpha}$ and $\tilde{\beta}$ of α and β. H is rejected if

$$\text{(5.1)}\qquad \tilde{M} = n(\tilde{\alpha},\,\tilde{\beta})\|\tau_{kl}\|_n^{-1}(\tilde{\alpha},\,\tilde{\beta})'$$

is too large, where $\|\tau_{kl}\|_n^{-1}$ is the inverse of $\|\tau_{kl}\|_n$ defined by

$$(5.2)\quad \tau_{11} = \tau_1^2 = (\textstyle\sum_j x_j^2)/\sum_j(x_j - \bar{x}_n)^2; \qquad \tau_2^2 = \{n^{-1}\textstyle\sum_j(x_j - \bar{x}_n)^2\}^{-1};$$

$$\tau_{21} = \tau_{12} = -\bar{x}_n/n^{-1}\textstyle\sum_j(x_j - \bar{x}_n)^2.$$

If, as is usual in classical tests, the distribution function F is assumed to be Φ, the normal df, then the estimates $\tilde{\alpha}$ and $\tilde{\beta}$ being linear functions of normal random variables, are themselves normal random variables, so that, under H, $\tilde{M}$ has a central χ^2 distribution with 2 degrees of freedom. And under any given alternative of the form $\alpha = a$, $\beta = b$, $\tilde{M}$ has a non-central χ^2 distribution with 2 degrees of freedom, and non-centrality parameter given by (see e.g. Lehmann [16], p. 284)

$$\tilde{\Delta}_n^2 = n(a + b\bar{x}_n)^2 + b\textstyle\sum_j(x_j - \bar{x}_n)^2.$$

It follows that under the sequence of alternatives K_n, the non-centrality parameter reduces to

$$(5.3)\qquad \tilde{\Delta}^2 = \lim\,(a^2 + 2ab\bar{x}_n + b^2n^{-1}\textstyle\sum_j x_j^2).$$

For any distribution function $F \varepsilon \mathfrak{F}$, the limit distribution of $\tilde{M}$ will still be χ^2, this is a consequence of theorem of Eicker [7], which gives general conditions for the least squares estimates to be asymptotically normally distributed. It can be verified [1] that Eicker's conditions are implied by our general assumptions of Section 1. We summarize the above facts in

LEMMA 5.1 *Under the assumptions of Lemma* 4.1, $\mathfrak{L}(\tilde{M} \mid P_n) \to \mathfrak{L}(\chi_2^2(\tilde{\Delta}^2))$ *where* $\chi_2^2\,(\tilde{\Delta}^2)$ *denotes the non-central chi-square random variable with* 2 *degrees of freedom and non-centrality parameter* $\tilde{\Delta}^2$ *given by* (5.3).

From (4.11) and (5.3), it follows that the asymptotic efficiency of the M-tests relative to the classical $\tilde{M}$-test is given by

$$(\textstyle\int_0^1 \psi(u)\varphi(u)\,du)^2/(\int_0^1 \psi^2(u)\,du).$$

If the common variance of the Y_j is σ_0^2, instead of unity, as we assumed, the efficiency becomes

$$(5.4)\qquad e_{M,\tilde{M}}(\psi) = \sigma_0^2(\textstyle\int_0^1 \psi(u)\varphi(u)\,du)^2/(\int_0^1 \psi^2(u)\,du).$$

On taking $\psi(u) = u$ (Wilcoxon), the efficiency expression on the right hand side of (5.4) reduces, after integration by parts, to

$$(5.5)\qquad e_{Mw.\tilde{M},}(F) = 12\sigma_0^2(\textstyle\int_{-\infty}^{\infty} f^2(y)\,dy)^2,$$

and on choosing $\psi(u) = \Phi^{-1}(\frac{1}{2}u + \frac{1}{2})$ (Van der Waerden) the efficiency simplifies to

$$(5.6)\qquad e_{Mn\cdot sc.\tilde{M},}(F) = \sigma_0^2 \textstyle\int_{-\infty}^{\infty} f^2(y)\,dy/\Phi'(\Phi^{-1}(F(y)))$$

where Φ' is the density of the standard normal distribution. Another special case of interest is obtained by taking $\psi(u) = \text{sign}\,u = 1$. The efficiency, in this case, becomes

$$(5.7)\qquad e_{Ms,\tilde{M}}(F) = 4\sigma_0^2 f^2(0).$$

We recognize (5.5) and (5.6) as the efficiencies of the Wilcoxon and the normal scores tests for shift relative to the t-test. Efficiency (5.5) has been studied in detail by Hodges and Lehmann [13], and (5.6) by Chernoff and Savage [3]. The question of choice between M_w and $M_{n.sc}$ as test statistics has been fully discussed in [14]. In general, provided the functions ψ and φ are non-decreasing on $(0, 1)$, the efficiency expression in (5.4) is the same as that of the corresponding rank score tests relative to the student's t-test or the F-test in the one sample [8] or the c-sample [20] problem. This is an immediate consequence of the similarity between the Chernoff-Savage $J(u)$ function used in [20], and Hájek's $\varphi(u)$ and $\psi(u)$ functions.

In [6] Daniels proposed a distribution-free test for H which is related to the Hodges' bivariate sign test [12] for symmetry. It would be of interest to compare Daniels' test and the M-tests with respect to their efficiency behaviour, but such a comparison does not seem to be readily feasible because the asymptotic distribution of Daniels' test under a sequence of alternatives is not known.

6. Acknowledgment. I should like to thank Professor Erich Lehmann, for his continued guidance and encouragement and Professor. J. Hájek for many helpful discussions, during the preparation of the dissertation [1], on which the present paper is based. I should also like to thank the referee for valuable suggestions.

REFERENCES

[1] ADICHIE, J. N. (1966) Unpublished Ph.D. Dissertation. University of California, Berkeley.

[2] ANDREWS, F. C.(1954) Asymptotic behaviour of some rank tests for analysis of variance. *Ann. Math. Statist.* **25** 724–735.

[3] CHERNOFF, H. and SAVAGE, I. R. (1958) Asymptotic normality and efficiency of certain non-parametric test statistics. *Ann. Math. Statist.* **29** 972–994.

[4] CRAMÉR, H. (1945) *Mathematical Methods of Statistics.* Princeton Univ. Press.

[5] CRAMÉR, H. (1963) *Random Variables and Probability Distributions* (2nd edition). Cambridge Univ. Press.

[6] DANIELS, H. E. (1954) A distribution-free test for regression parameters. *Ann. Math. Statist.* **25** 499–513.

[7] EICKER, F. (1963) Asymptotic normality and consistency of the least squares estimators for families of linear regressions. *Ann. Math. Statist.* **34** 447–456.

[8] GOVINDARAJULU, Z. (1960) Central limits theorems and asymptotic efficiency for one sample non-parametric procedures. Technical Report No. 11, Univ. of Minnesota

[9] HÁJEK, J. (1961) Some extensions of the Wald-Wolfowitz-Noether theorem. *Ann. Math. Statist.* **32** 506–523.

[10] HÁJEK, J. (1962) Asymptotically most powerful rank order tests. *Ann. Math. Statist.* **33** 1124–1147.

[11] HANNAN, E. J. (1956) The asymptotic power of tests based on multiple correlation. *J. Roy. Statist. Soc. Ser. B* **18** 227–233.

[12] HILL, B. M. (1960) A relation between Hodges bivariate sign test and a non-parametric test of Daniels. *Ann. Math. Statist.* **31** 1190–1196.

[13] HODGES, J. L., JR. and LEHMANN, E. L. (1956) Efficiency of some non-parametric competitors of the t-test. *Ann. Math. Statist.* **27** 324–335.

[14] Hodges, J. L., Jr. and Lehmann, E. L. (1961) Comparison of the normal scores and Wilcoxon tests. *Proc. Fourth Berk. Symp. Math. Statist. Prob.* **1** 307–317. Univ. of California Press.

[15] LeCam, L. (1960) Locally asymptotic normal families of distribution. *Univ. of California Publ. Statist.* **3** No. 2 37–98.

[16] Lehmann, E. L. (1959) *Testing Statistical Hypotheses.* Wiley, New York.

[17] Loève, M. (1962) *Probability Theory* (3rd edition). Van Nostrand, New York.

[18] Mood, A. M. (1950) *Introduction to the Theory of Statistics.* McGraw-Hill, New York.

[19] Noether, G. E. (1954) On a theorem of Pitman. *Ann. Math. Statist.* **25** 514–522.

[20] Puri, M. L. (1964) Asymptotic efficiency of a class of c-Sample tests. *Ann. Math. Statist.* **35** 102–121.

[21] Sverdrup, E. (1952) The limit distribution of a continuous function of random variables. *Skand. Akturaietidskrift.* **35** 1–10.

This article above was written by Prof. James Adichie and published in 1967.

ESTIMATES OF REGRESSION PARAMETERS BASED ON RANK TESTS[1]

By J. N. Adichie

University of Nigeria, Nsukka

0. Introduction and summary. In the linear regression model $Y_j = \alpha + \beta x_j + Z_j$, it is usual to estimate α and β by the method of least squares. This method has, among other things, the nice property of providing "best" linear unbiased estimates, under very general conditions. Various other methods of estimation of the parameters are well known, see for example [12] and [14]. Most of these methods however make use of the actual values of the observations, and the estimates they yield are generally vulnerable to gross errors. For some alternative approaches to the problem, see [7], [11] and [13].

In a recent paper [9], Hodges and Lehmann proposed a general method of obtaining robust point estimates for the location parameter, from statistics used to test the hypothesis that this parameter has a specified value. In Section 1 of this paper, this method is used to define point estimates $\hat{\alpha}$ and $\hat{\beta}$ of α and β, in terms of certain test statistics. It is shown that the least squares estimates are obtainable as special cases from the general method of estimation discussed. In Section 2, the existence of 'rank score' estimates is proved, and in Section 3, computing techniques are given and illustrated with an example. Both the small sample and asymptotic properties of the estimates are discussed. It is shown, for example, that the joint distribution of the estimates $\hat{\alpha}$ and $\hat{\beta}$ is symmetric with respect to the parameter point (α, β)—and hence that $\hat{\alpha}$ and $\hat{\beta}$ are unbiased—if the underlying distribution of the observations is symmetric. In Section 5, the joint asymptotic normality of $\hat{\alpha}$ and $\hat{\beta}$ is proved, and in Section 6, it is shown that the asymptotic efficiency of $(\hat{\alpha}, \hat{\beta})$ is the same as the Pitman efficiency of the rank tests [1], on which they are based, relative to the classical tests. Finally in Section 7, the $(\hat{\alpha}, \hat{\beta})$-estimates are compared with the Brown and Mood median estimates with respect to their efficiencies.

1. Estimation of α and β. As in [1], let $Y_1, \cdots, Y_n$ be independent random variables with distributions

$$P_{\alpha\beta}(Y_j \leqq y) = F(y - \alpha - \beta x_j) \tag{1.1}$$

where x_j are the known regression constants that are not all equal and which satisfy the limiting conditions given in [1], and $P_{\alpha\beta}$ denotes the probability computed for the parameter values α and β. As before we shall assume that the underlying distribution function F belongs to a class $\mathfrak{F}$ of absolutely continuous

Received 1 September 1966; revised 30 January 1967.

[1] This research was based in part on the author's Ph.D. dissertation submitted to the University of California, Berkeley; and was prepared with the partial support of the Agency for International Development under contract MSU AIDc-1398, and of the National Science Foundation, Grant GP-5059.

symmetric distribution functions, the densities of which are also absolutely continuous and square integrable. With these regularity conditions, we shall define estimates $\hat{\alpha}$ and $\hat{\beta}$ which are similar to the Hodges and Lehmann estimates for shift [9].

Let $T_1(Y_1, \cdots, Y_n)$ and $T_2(Y_1, \cdots, Y_n)(T_1(Y)$ and $T_2(Y)$ for short) be two statistics for testing hypotheses about α and β in (1.1). Assume that T_1 and T_2 satisfy the following two conditions:

(A) for fixed b, $T_1(y + a + bx)$ is non-decreasing in a; and for every a, $T_2(y + a + bx)$ is non-decreasing in b, for each y and x. Here $y + a + bx$ stands for $(y_1 + a + bx_1, \cdots, y_n + a + bx_n)$.

(B) When $\alpha = \beta = 0$, the distributions of $T_1(Y)$ and $T_2(Y)$ are symmetric about fixed points μ and ν, independent of $F \varepsilon \mathfrak{F}$.

Let

$$(1.2) \qquad \beta^* = \sup \{b: T_2(y - a - bx) > \nu, \text{ for all } a\},$$

$$\beta^{**} = \inf \{b: T_2(y - a - bx) < \nu, \text{ for all } a\};$$

$$(1.3) \qquad \hat{\beta} = \tfrac{1}{2}(\beta^* + \beta^{**});$$

$$(1.4) \qquad \alpha^* = \sup \{a: T_1(y - a - \hat{\beta}x) > \mu\},$$

$$\alpha^{**} = \inf \{a: T_1(y - a - \hat{\beta}x) < \mu\};$$

$$(1.5) \qquad \hat{\alpha} = \tfrac{1}{2}(\alpha^* + \alpha^{**}).$$

For suitable functions T_1 and T_2, we propose $\hat{\alpha}$ and $\hat{\beta}$ as estimates of α and β.

It may be remarked that many existing estimates of α and β, belong to the class of (1.3)- and (1.5)-estimates. In particular, the least squares estimates $\tilde{\alpha}$ and $\tilde{\beta}$ are obtainable as special cases of $\hat{\alpha}$ and $\hat{\beta}$. To see this, take $T_1(Y) = \sum_j Y_j$ and $T_2(Y) = \sum_j (x_j - \bar{x}_n)(Y_j - \bar{Y}_n)$ where as before $\bar{x}_n = n^{-1} \sum_j x_j$, and all the summations are from 1 to n. With these choices of the functions T_1 and T_2, it is easy to see that conditions (A) and (B) are satisfied with $\mu = \nu = 0$. Furthermore,

$$\sup \{b: T_2(y - a - bx) > 0, \text{ for all } a\}$$

$$(1.6) \qquad = \inf \{b: T_2(y - a - bx) < 0, \text{ for all } a\}$$

$$= \{\textstyle\sum_j (x_j - x_n)(y_j - \bar{y}_n)\}/\{\textstyle\sum_j (x_j - \bar{x}_n)^2\} = \tilde{\beta}.$$

In the same way,

$$(1.7) \qquad \sup \{a: T_1(y - a - \tilde{\beta}x) > 0\} = \inf \{a: T_1(y - a - \tilde{\beta}x) < 0\}$$

$$= (\bar{y}_n - \tilde{\beta}\bar{x}_n) = \tilde{\alpha}.$$

2. Estimates based on rank tests. Since our main interest is in robust estimates, we shall be primarily concerned with $\hat{\alpha}$ and $\hat{\beta}$ based on rank (or mixed rank) statistics. As in [1], we shall need the following functions:

$$(2.1) \qquad \psi(u) = -[g'(G^{-1}(\tfrac{1}{2}u + \tfrac{1}{2}))/g(G^{-1}(\tfrac{1}{2}u + \tfrac{1}{2}))], \qquad 0 < u < 1,$$

(2.2) $\psi_0(u) = -[g'(G^{-1}(u)/g(G^{-1}(u))], \qquad 0 < u < 1,$

(2.3) $\varphi_0(u) = -[f'(F^{-1}(u))/f(F^{-1}(u))], \qquad 0 < u < 1,$

where G^{-1} is the inverse of G, and G is any distribution function belonging to the class $\mathfrak{F}$. Consider the following pair of statistics:

(2.4) $T_1(Y) = n^{-1}\sum_j \psi_n(\mathfrak{R}_j/n + 1) \text{ Sign } Y_j$

and

(2.5) $T_2(Y) = n^{-1}\sum_j(x_j - \bar{x}_n)\psi_{0n}(R_j/n + 1)$

where $\mathfrak{R}_j$ is the rank of $|Y_j|$ in the sequence of absolute values $|Y_1|, \cdots, |Y_n|$ of the n observations, while R_j is the rank of Y_j in the ordered sample $V_1 < \cdots < V_n$, i.e. $Y_j = V_{R_j}, j = 1, \cdots, n$, and

(2.6) $\psi_n(u) = \psi(j/n + 1),$

$\psi_{0n}(u) = \psi_0(j/n + 1) \quad \text{for} \quad (j - 1)/n < u \leqq j/n.$

Observe that the statistic T_1 of (2.4) is the same as the one studied in [1], while T_2 of (2.5) is studied by Hájek [6]. It can be shown by arguments similar to those in [9], that with (2.4) and (2.5) as choices for T_1 and T_2, conditions (A) and (B) are satisfied, and hence that the estimates based on them, exist and are well defined. If in (2.1) and (2.2) we choose G to be the logistic distribution function, then $\psi(u)$ becomes u and $T_1(Y)$ and $T_2(Y)$ of (2.4) and (2.5) coincide with the Wilcoxon one-sample and two-sample statistics respectively. Denoting by $\hat{\alpha}_w$ and $\hat{\beta}_w$ the resulting estimates, we then have that

(2.7) $T_1(y - a - \hat{\beta}_w x) = [n(n + 1)]^{-1}\sum_j \hat{\mathfrak{R}}_j \text{ Sign } (y_j - a - \hat{\beta}_w x_j)$

$= [n(n + 1)]^{-1}[2N^+ - n(n + 1)/2]$

where N^+ is the number of pairs (i, j) with $1 \leqq i \leqq j \leqq n$, such that $y_i + y_j - \hat{\beta}_w(x_i + x_j) - 2a$ is positive, and $\hat{\mathfrak{R}}_j$ is the rank of $|y_j - a - \hat{\beta}_w x_j|$ in the sequence of absolute values $|y_1 - a - \hat{\beta}_w x_1|, \cdots, |y_n - a - \hat{\beta}_w x_n|$. The estimate $\hat{\alpha}_w$ is then given by

(2.8) $\hat{\alpha}_w = \text{med}_{i \leqq j} \tfrac{1}{2}\{Y_i + Y_j - \hat{\beta}_w(x_i + x_j)\},$

where $\hat{\beta}_w$ is obtained from (1.2) and (1.3) with

(2.9) $T_2(Y) = n^{-1}\sum_j(x_j - \bar{x}_n)(R_j/n + 1).$

3. Computation of the Wilcoxon estimate $\hat{\beta}_w$. An explicit expression, for $\hat{\beta}_w$ in terms of Y's does not seem to be available, without restrictive assumptions on the regression constants x_j. As an example of such an assumption if we take

$$x_j = c_1, \qquad j = 1, \cdots, k,$$
$$= c_2, \qquad j = k + 1, \cdots, n,$$

the estimate $\hat{\beta}_w$ so obtained would coincide with the Hodges and Lehmann estimate for shift in the two-sample problem, i.e. $\hat{\beta}_w = \text{med}\,(Y - Z)$ where $Y = (Y_1, \cdots, Y_k)$ and $Z = (Y_{k+1}, \cdots, Y_n)$. However for any given constants x_j an iterative method may be used to compute $\hat{\beta}_w$, for moderate sample size n. The procedure described below depends mainly on the monotonicity of $T_2(y + bx)$ as a function of b. There are however some values of b, for which ties occur. For any such b we define

$$(3.1) \quad T_2(y + bx) = \tfrac{1}{2}[\sup_{b'<b} T_2(y + b'x) + \inf_{b'>b} T_2(y + b'x)].$$

Note that the use of mid-ranks is not acceptable here for it badly dislocates the monotonicity of $T_2(y + bx)$.

Let $y_1, \cdots, y_n$ be the values of the observations, taken at levels $x_1, \cdots, x_n$, respectively. Choose any b_0 for which there is no tie, (usually $b_0 = 0$ for a start) and rank the n differences $y_j - b_0x_j$, $j = 1, \cdots, n$. Then compute $T_2(y - b_0x)$. If the result is positive (negative) increase (decrease) b_0 to b_1 and compute $T_2(y - b_1x)$. Continue this iteration increasing (decreasing) b at each step until $T_2(y - bx)$ becomes zero. The b-value that achieves this would be the estimate. If $T_2(y - bx) = 0$ for $b' \leq b \leq b''$, then the estimate would be $\frac{1}{2}(b' + b'')$. If on the other hand, $T_2(y - bx)$ does not assume the value zero, there would be, by condition (A), a certain b_0 say, such that for $b > b_0$, $T_2(y - bx) < 0$, while for $b < b_0$, $T_2(y - bx) > 0$.

In such a case b_0 would be the estimate. To find b_0, continue the iteration described above, in close steps of b, until $T_2(y - bx)$ changes sign. Then go back and forth to determine where the first change of sign occurs.

Example. Consider the following set of data, taken from Graybill's *Introduction to Linear Statistical Models* Vol. 1.

x	1	2	3	4	10	12	18
y	9	15	19	20	45	55	78

The results of the iterative method described above, are set out below in the form of Tables 3.1(a) and 3.1(b). The estimate $\hat{\beta}_w$ obtained from the tables has the value 4.00 while the corresponding least squares estimate $\tilde{\beta}$ has the value 4.02. Observe that for $b = 4.00$, $T_2(y - bx)$ is defined by (3.1).

4. Invariance and symmetry properties. As in [9], the estimates $\hat{\alpha}$ and $\hat{\beta}$ have useful invariance and symmetry properties in a sense to be made precise in the following two lemmas.

Lemma 4.1. *For any real a and b, the* (1.3)- *and* (1.5)-*estimates possess the following translation invariant properties:*

$$(4.1) \qquad \hat{\beta}(y + a + bx) = \hat{\beta}(y) + b$$

and

$$(4.2) \qquad \hat{\alpha}(y + a + bx) = \hat{\alpha}(y) + a.$$

Proof. (4.1) is immediate from definition (1.3) while (4.2) follows from (4.1) and (1.5).

TABLE 3.1(a)

b		$x = 1$	2	3	4	10	12	18
$b = 0$	$(y - bx) =$	9	15	19	20	45	55	78
	ranks =	1	2	3	4	5	6	7
$b = 2.0$	$(y - bx) =$	7	11	13	12	25	31	42
	rank =	1	2	4	3	5	6	7
$b = 3.0$	$(y - bx) =$	6	9	10	8	15	19	30
	rank =	1	3	4	2	5	6	7
$b = 3.99$	$(y - bx) =$	5.01	7.02	7.03	4.04	5.1	7.12	6.18
	ranks =	2	5	6	1	3	7	4
$b = 4.01$	$(y - bx) =$	4.99	6.98	6.97	3.96	4.9	6.86	5.82
	ranks =	3	7	6	1	2	5	4

TABLE 3.1(b)

$b =$	0	2	3	3.99	4.01
$T_2(y - bx) =$	78.24	77.24	75.24	19.80	−9.14

$\hat{\beta}_w = 4.00.$

From (4.1) and (4.2) it follows that, for all real a and b,

$$(4.3) \qquad P_{\alpha\beta}\{(\hat{\alpha} - \alpha), (\hat{\beta} - \beta) \leqq (a, b)\} = P_{00}\{(\hat{\alpha}, \hat{\beta}) \leqq (a, b)\}.$$

In computing the distributions of the estimates, we may therefore assume that $\alpha = \beta = 0$.

One would like to have the distributions of $\hat{\alpha}$ and $\hat{\beta}$, centered in some sense, on the true parameter values. The next lemma gives conditions under which $\hat{\alpha}$ and $\hat{\beta}$ are symmetrically distributed about α and β.

LEMMA 4.2. *Let $T_1(Y)$ and $T_2(Y)$ be given by (2.4) and (2.5), with ψ non-decreasing, and let $\hat{\alpha}$ and $\hat{\beta}$ be the (1.5) and (1.3)-estimates. If $F \varepsilon \mathfrak{F}$, then $\hat{\beta}$ is symmetrically distributed about β, and $\hat{\alpha}$ is symmetrically distributed about α, and hence $\hat{\alpha}$ and $\hat{\beta}$ are unbiased.*

PROOF. Similar to the proof of Theorem 2 of [9].

5. Limiting distributions. The study of the asymptotic distributions of $\hat{\alpha}$ and $\hat{\beta}$ is based on a result of Hodges and Lehmann (see Theorem 4 of [9]) which gives the connection between the distribution of the estimate and that of the test statistic, on which it is based. Using this result, it can be seen that, under the regularity conditions of Lemma 4.1 of [1],

$$(5.1) \quad \lim \mathfrak{L}(n^{\frac{1}{2}}(\hat{\beta} - \beta) \mid P_\beta) = \lim \mathfrak{L}(n^{\frac{1}{2}}\hat{\beta} \mid P_0) = N(0, k^2(\psi_0)/c^2)$$

where

$$(5.2) \qquad k^2(\psi_0) = k^2(\psi) = \left(\int_0^1 \psi^2(u)\, du\right) / \left(\int_0^1 \psi(u)\varphi(u)\, du\right)^2$$

with $c^2 = \lim n^{-1} \sum_j (x_j - \bar{x}_n)^2$, and $\varphi_0(u)$ is defined as in (2.3).

For the joint limiting distribution of $(\hat{\alpha}, \hat{\beta})$, it is convenient to consider first the asymptotic distribution of

$$\hat{\delta}_n = \hat{\alpha} + \hat{\beta}\bar{x}_n . \tag{5.3}$$

Observe that if we write the identity

$$Y_j = \alpha + \beta x_j + Z_j = \delta_n + \beta \xi_j + Z_j$$

where $\sum_j \xi_j = 0$, then δ_n depends on n only through a known quantity $\bar{x}_n$, and the estimate $\hat{\delta}_n$ of δ_n is still based on $T_1(Y - \hat{\beta}x)$. Furthermore, the invariance property (4.1) and (4.2) of the estimates, yield equation (5.3).

The following slight generalization of a result in [9], shall be used in the sequel.

THEOREM 5.1 (Hodges and Lehmann). *Let $\bar{x}_n \to \bar{x}$ as $n \to \infty$, and let*

$$\Delta_n = -n^{-\frac{1}{2}}(a + b) \tag{5.4}$$

where a and b are real constants. Let Φ be the distribution function of a normal random variable with mean zero and unit variance, and suppose

$$\lim P_n\{n^{\frac{1}{2}}T_1(Y) \leq y\} = \Phi[(y + dB)/A] \tag{5.5}$$

where $d = (a + b\bar{x})$, and P_n denotes that the probability is computed for the sequence of parameter values Δ_n. Then for any sequence

$$\delta_n = \alpha + \beta\bar{x}_n \text{ that tends to } \alpha + \beta\bar{x} = \delta, \tag{5.6}$$

$$\lim P_{\delta_n}\{n^{\frac{1}{2}}(\hat{\delta}_n - \delta_n) \leq d\} = \Phi(dB/A).$$

To establish the limiting distribution of $\hat{\delta}_n$, we need the asymptotic distribution under Δ_n of the statistic

$$n^{\frac{1}{2}}T_1(\hat{Z}) = n^{-\frac{1}{2}}\sum_j \psi_n(\hat{\mathfrak{R}}_j/n + 1) \text{ Sign } \hat{Z}_j \tag{5.7}$$

where $\hat{\mathfrak{R}}_j$ is the rank of $|\hat{Z}_j|$ in the sequence of absolute values $|\hat{Z}_1|, \cdots, |\hat{Z}_n|$, with $\hat{Z}_j = Y_j - \hat{\beta}x_j$.

This asymptotic distribution may be obtained by the help of the following theorem, the proof of which is given in the appendix.

THEOREM 5.2. *Let $\dot{\beta}$ be any estimate of β in (1.1) such that*

$$n^{\frac{1}{2}}(\dot{\beta} - \beta) \text{ is bounded in probability as } n \to \infty . \tag{5.8}$$

Assume that the regularity conditions of Lemma 4.1 of [1] are satisfied. If

$$|d/dy\psi(G(y))| \leq K(\text{a constant}), \tag{5.9}$$

then

$$\lim \mathfrak{L}(n^{\frac{1}{2}}T_1(\dot{Z}) \mid P_n) = \lim \mathfrak{L}(n^{\frac{1}{2}}T_1(Y) \mid P_n) \tag{5.10}$$

where $\dot{Z}_j = Y_j - \dot{\beta}x_j$, P_n denotes the distribution under Δ_n of (5.4).

We remark that (5.8) is satisfied by all the (1.3)-estimates based on (2.5); it can also be easily verified that (5.9) is satisfied by the usual symmetric distributions such as the normal, the double exponential and the logistic. It follows from Theorem 4.1 of [1], that under the assumptions of Theorem 5.2, $T_1(\hat{Z})$ and $T_2(Y)$ defined in (2.4) and (2.5) are asymptotically independent with limiting distributions

$$\lim \mathcal{L}(n^{\frac{1}{2}}T_1(\hat{Z}) \mid P_n) = N(d \textstyle\int \psi\varphi, \int \psi^2),$$
$$\lim \mathcal{L}(n^{\frac{1}{2}}T_2(Y) \mid P_n) = N(b \textstyle\int \psi_0\varphi_0, c^2 \int \psi_0^2),$$

hence $\hat{\delta}_n$ and $\hat{\beta}$ are asymptotically independent with the limiting distribution of $\hat{\delta}_n$ given by

$$(5.11) \quad \lim \mathcal{L}(n^{\frac{1}{2}}(\hat{\delta}_n - \delta_n) \mid P_{\delta_n}) = \lim \mathcal{L}(n^{\frac{1}{2}}\hat{\delta}_n \mid P_0) = N(0, k^2(\psi))$$

where $k^2(\psi)$ is defined in (5.2).

To compute the limiting distribution of $(\hat{\alpha}, \hat{\beta})$, we use the following simple lemma.

LEMMA 5.1. *Let (X_n, Y_n) be a sequence of random vectors and $\{u_n\}$, $\{v_n\}$ be two sequences of constants, such that $u_n \to u$, $v_n \to v$ as $n \to \infty$. If* $\lim \mathcal{L}(X_n, Y_n) = \mathcal{L}(X, Y)$, *then* $\lim \mathcal{L}(u_nX_n + v_nY_n, Y_n) = \mathcal{L}(uX + vY, Y)$.

With this lemma, it is straight forward to establish the following main result of this section.

THEOREM 5.3. *Let $\hat{\alpha}$ and $\hat{\beta}$ be the (1.5)- and (1.3)-estimates based on (2.4) and (2.5) respectively. Assume that the regularity conditions of Theorem 5.2 are satisfied. Then $\mathcal{L}(n^{\frac{1}{2}}(\hat{\alpha} - \alpha, \hat{\beta} - \beta) \mid P_{\alpha\beta})$ tends to the bivariate normal distribution with means (0, 0) and covariance matrix $k^2(\psi)\Sigma$, where*

$$(5.12) \qquad \Sigma = \begin{pmatrix} (c^2 + \bar{x}^2)/c^2 & -\bar{x}/c^2 \\ -\bar{x}/c^2 & 1/c^2 \end{pmatrix}$$

with $c^2 = \lim n^{-1}\sum_j (x_j - \bar{x}_n)^2$, *and* $\bar{x} = \lim \bar{x}_n$.

6. Asymptotic efficiency. In this section, we determine the asymptotic efficiency of our estimates relative to the classical least squares estimates. In doing this, we make use of the fact that if two vectors $\mathbf{U}_1$ and $\mathbf{U}_2$ have limiting normal distributions with covariance matrices Σ_1 and Σ_2 related by $\Sigma_1 = k^2\Sigma_2$, for some constant k, then the asymptotic efficiency of $\mathbf{U}_2$ relative to $\mathbf{U}_1$ is k^2.

Conditions for the asymptotic normality of a general class of least squares estimates have been given by Eicker [5]. It can easily be checked that under the assumptions of Theorem 5.2, the conditions in [5] are satisfied. If $\tilde{\alpha}$ and $\tilde{\beta}$ denote the least squares estimates then under very general conditions, $\mathcal{L}(n^{\frac{1}{2}}(\tilde{\alpha} - \alpha, \tilde{\beta} - \beta) \mid P_{\alpha\beta})$ tends to the bivariate normal distribution with zero mean and covariance matrix Σ given in (5.12). It follows that the asymptotic efficiency of the estimates $(\hat{\alpha}, \hat{\beta}) = \hat{\mathbf{\Delta}}$ relative to the least squares estimates $(\tilde{\alpha}, \tilde{\beta}) = \tilde{\mathbf{\Delta}}$ is $k^{-2}(\psi)$. If the common variance of Y_j is σ^2 instead of unity as assumed, the efficiency becomes

$$(6.1) \qquad e_{\hat{\mathbf{\Delta}}, \tilde{\mathbf{\Delta}}}(\psi) = \sigma^2\left(\textstyle\int_0^1 \psi(u)\varphi(u)\,du\right)^2 / \left(\int_0^1 \psi^2(u)\,du\right).$$

As expected, (6.1) is the same as the Pitman efficiency [1] of the M_n-tests relative to the classical F-test. This is unlike the situation in the multivariate location case where the corresponding efficiencies do not coincide, see Bickel [2] and [3]. From the particular cases of (6.1) discussed in [1], it follows that the estimates $\hat{\alpha}$ and $\hat{\beta}$ have all the desirable properties including robustness [10], of the Hodges and Lehmann estimates for shift.

7. Comparison with the Brown and Mood Estimates. In [11], Brown and Mood proposed the 'median' estimates $\dot{\alpha}$ and $\dot{\beta}$ of α and β. These estimates are determined by the two equations:

$$\text{Median } (Y_j - \dot{\alpha} - \dot{\beta} x_j) = 0 \quad \text{for} \quad x_j \leqq \text{med } x, \tag{7.1}$$

$$\text{Median } (Y_i - \dot{\alpha} - \dot{\beta} x_i) = 0 \quad \text{for} \quad x_i > \text{med } x, \tag{7.2}$$

where med x is the median of the constants x_j, $j = 1, \cdots, n$.

In [8] Hill proved both the existence and the asymptotic normality of $(\dot{\alpha}, \dot{\beta}) = \dot{\mathbf{\Delta}}$. He showed that $\mathfrak{L}((\tfrac{1}{2}n)^{\frac{1}{2}}(\dot{\alpha} - \alpha, \dot{\beta} - \beta))$ tends to the bivariate normal distribution with mean (0, 0) and covariance matrix $\|\tau_{\alpha\beta}\|$ defined by

$$\tau_\alpha^2 = [(\textstyle\int_0^{\frac{1}{2}} h(t)\, dt)^2 + (\int_{\frac{1}{2}}^1 h(t)\, dt)^2](2f^2(\theta)\{\int_{\frac{1}{2}}^1 h(t)\, dt - \int_0^{\frac{1}{2}} h(t)\, dt\}^2)^{-1}, \tag{7.3}$$

$$\tau_\beta^2 = \{8[f(0)\{\textstyle\int_{\frac{1}{2}}^1 h(t)\, dt - \int_0^{\frac{1}{2}} h(t)\, dt\}]^2\}^{-1}, \tag{7.4}$$

$$\tau_{\alpha\beta} = -\textstyle\int_0^1 h(t)\, dt\{8[f(0)\{\int_{\frac{1}{2}}^1 h(t)\, dt - \int_0^{\frac{1}{2}} h(t)\, dt\}]^2\}^{-1}, \tag{7.5}$$

where h is a continuous strictly monotone increasing function on [0, 1] (also called spacing function) defined by

$$x_{nj} = h(j/n), \qquad j = 0, \cdots, n. \tag{7.6}$$

Since the asymptotic covariance matrix of $\dot{\mathbf{\Delta}}$ is not proportional to that of $\hat{\mathbf{\Delta}}$, in order to compute their efficiencies one may use another measure of efficiency based on asymptotic generalized variance (Cramér [4], p. 301).

The asymptotic generalized variance of $n^{\frac{1}{2}}\dot{\mathbf{\Delta}}$ is

$$\text{Var } n^{\frac{1}{2}}\dot{\mathbf{\Delta}} = [4f^2(0)\{\textstyle\int_{\frac{1}{2}}^1 h(t)\, dt - \int_0^{\frac{1}{2}} h(t)\, dt\}]^{-2}, \tag{7.7}$$

and that of the (1.3)- and (1.5)- estimates $\hat{\mathbf{\Delta}}$ is

$$\text{Var } n^{\frac{1}{2}}\hat{\mathbf{\Delta}} = [\textstyle\int_0^1 \psi^2(u)\, du]^2/[c^2\{\int_0^1 \psi(u)\varphi(u)\, du\}]. \tag{7.8}$$

It therefore follows that the asymptotic efficiency of the median estimates $\dot{\mathbf{\Delta}}$ relative to the $\hat{\mathbf{\Delta}}$-estimates is given by

$$e_{\dot{\mathbf{\Delta}},\hat{\mathbf{\Delta}}} = [f^2(0)\{\textstyle\int_{\frac{1}{2}}^1 h(t)\, dt - \int_0^{\frac{1}{2}} h(t)\, dt\} \int_0^1 \psi^2(u)\, du] \cdot\{[\int_0^1 \psi(u)\varphi(u)\, du]^2[\int_0^1 h^2(t)\, dt - (\int_0^1 h(t)\, dt)^2]^{\frac{1}{2}}\}^{-1} \tag{7.9}$$

where we have written c in terms of the function h, by the relation $\lim n^{-1}\sum_j x_j = \int_0^1 h(t)\, dt$. If we consider in particular the estimates $(\hat{\alpha}_s, \hat{\beta}_s) = \hat{\mathbf{\Delta}}_s$, based on the sign statistics $T_1(Y) = n^{-1}\sum_j \text{Sign } Y_j$ and $T_2(Y) = n^{-1}\sum_j (x_j - \bar{x}) \text{ Sign } Y_j$, the efficiency expression in (7.9) reduces to

$$e_{\dot{\mathbf{\Delta}},\hat{\mathbf{\Delta}}_s} = [\textstyle\int_{\frac{1}{2}}^1 h(t)\, dt - \int_0^{\frac{1}{2}} h(t)\, dt][\int_0^1 h^2(t)\, dt - (\int_0^1 h(t)\, dt)^2]^{-\frac{1}{2}}. \tag{7.10}$$

The function h is typically linear with positive slope, and with this, (7.10) simplifies to

$$e_{\hat{\Delta},\hat{\Delta}^s} = 3^{\frac{1}{2}}/2 < 1 \tag{7.11}$$

which implies that there is some loss in the efficiency of the median estimates. This loss is probably due to the fact that some information is lost in the process of ordering the observations in two separate groups.

APPENDIX

8. Proof of Theorem 5.2. Throughout this section, k will denote a generic constant and θ_j (short for $\theta_{nj}(t)$) a generic sequence of functions that tends to zero uniformly in t for $|t| \leq k$, as $n \to \infty$.

Let $Y_j^* = Y_j - n^{\frac{1}{2}}(tx_j)$ for $|t| \leq k$ and let E_0 denote the expectation taken with respect to the distribution under $\alpha = \beta = 0$. Write

$$(8.1) \qquad T_1(Y) = n^{-1} \textstyle\sum_j \psi_n(\mathcal{R}_j/n + 1) \text{ Sign } Y_j ,$$
$$T_1(Y^*) = n^{-1} \textstyle\sum_j \psi_n(\mathcal{R}_j^*/n + 1) \text{ Sign } Y_j^*,$$

where $\mathcal{R}_j^*$ is the rank of $|Y_j^*|$ in the sequence of absolute values $|Y_1^*|, \cdots, |Y_n^*|$.

Due to the independence of $(\mathcal{R}_1, \cdots, \mathcal{R}_n)$ and $(\text{Sign } Y_1, \cdots, \text{Sign } Y_n)$.

$$\begin{aligned}\text{Var}_0\,[n^{\frac{1}{2}}(T_1 - T_1^*)] &= n\{E_0(T_1 - T_1^*)^2 - [E_0(T_1 - T_1^*)]^2\} \\ &= n^{-1} \textstyle\sum_j E_0[\psi_n(\mathcal{R}_j^*/n + 1) \text{ Sign } Y_j^* - \psi_n(\mathcal{R}_j/n + 1) \text{ Sign } Y_j]^2 \\ &\qquad - n^{-1}[\textstyle\sum_j E_0\{\psi_n(\mathcal{R}_j^*/n + 1) \text{ Sign } Y_j^*\}]^2 \\ &\leq n^{-1} \textstyle\sum_j E_0[\psi_n(\mathcal{R}_j^*/n + 1) \text{ Sign } Y_j^* - \psi_n(\mathcal{R}_j/n + 1) \text{ Sign } Y_j]^2 \\ &= B_1 + B_2 + B_3 ,\end{aligned}$$

with

$$B_1 = n^{-1} \textstyle\sum_j E_0[\psi_n(\mathcal{R}_j^*/n + 1) - \psi_n(\mathcal{R}_j/n + 1)]^2,$$
$$B_2 = n^{-1} \textstyle\sum_j E_0[\psi_n(\mathcal{R}_j^*/n + 1)(\text{Sign } Y_j^* - \text{Sign } Y_j)]^2,$$
$$\begin{aligned}B_3 = 2n^{-1} \textstyle\sum_j E_0[\{\psi_n(\mathcal{R}_j^*/n + 1) - \psi_n(\mathcal{R}_j/n + 1)\}\{\text{Sign } Y_j^*\} \\ \cdot\{\psi_n(\mathcal{R}_j^*/n + 1)\}\{\text{Sign } Y_j^* - \text{Sign } Y_j\}].\end{aligned}$$

Now

$$\begin{aligned}|B_2| &= 4\,|n^{-1} \textstyle\sum_j \{(tx_j)/n^{\frac{1}{2}}\} f(\theta_j) E_0\psi_n^2(\mathcal{R}_j^*/n + 1)| \\ &\leq \max_{1 \leq j \leq n} k\,|n^{-\frac{1}{2}} x_j f(\theta_j)|\; n^{-1} \textstyle\sum_j \psi_n^2(j/n + 1).\end{aligned}$$

Using the absolute continuity of f, and the boundedness of the regression constants x_j (see (1.2), (1.3) and (1.4) of [1]), we see that $\lim_n \sup_t |B_2| = 0$. For B_3, we have

$$|B_3| = |2n^{-1} \sum_j E_0[\psi_n^2(\mathfrak{R}_j^*/n+1) - \psi_n(\mathfrak{R}_j/n+1)\psi_n(\mathfrak{R}_j^*/n+1)] \cdot [1 - \text{Sign } Y_j \text{ Sign } Y_j^*]|$$

$$\leq \max_{1 \leq j \leq n} k\, |n^{-\frac{1}{2}} x_j f(\theta_j)|\, n^{-1} \sum_j |E_0[\psi_n^2(\mathfrak{R}_j^*/n+1) - \psi_n(\mathfrak{R}_j/n+1)\psi_n(\mathfrak{R}_j^*/n+1)]|$$

$$\leq \max_{1 \leq j \leq n} k\, |n^{-\frac{1}{2}} x_j f(\theta_j)|\, n^{-1} \sum_j \psi^2(j/n+1).$$

Hence $\lim_n \sup_t |B_3| = 0$ for $|t| \leq k$. Write $B_1 = \sum_{i=1}^{6} B_{1i}$, where

$$B_{11} = n^{-1} \sum_j E_0[\psi_n(\mathfrak{R}_j/n+1) - \psi(U_j)]^2,$$
$$B_{12} = n^{-1} \sum_j E_0[\psi_n(\mathfrak{R}_j^*/n+1) - \psi(U_j^*)]^2,$$
$$B_{13} = n^{-1} \sum_j E_0[\psi(U_j) - \psi(U_j^*)]^2,$$
$$B_{14} = 2n^{-1} \sum_j E_0[\psi_n(\mathfrak{R}_j/n+1) - \psi(U_j)][\psi(U_j^*) - \psi_n(\mathfrak{R}_j^*/n+1)],$$
$$B_{15} = 2n^{-1} \sum_j E_0[\psi_n(\mathfrak{R}_j/n+1) - \psi(U_j)][\psi(U_j) - \psi(U_j^*)],$$
$$B_{16} = 2n^{-1} \sum_j E_0[\psi(U_j^*) - \psi_n(\mathfrak{R}_j^*/n+1)][\psi(U_j) - \psi(U_j^*)],$$

where $U_j = 2F(Y_j) - 1$, $U_j^* = 2F(Y_j^*) - 1$.

By (2.4) of [1], it is immediate that both B_{11} and B_{12} tend to zero uniformly in t for $|t| \leq k$. On applying the mean value theorem to B_{13}, we obtain

$$|B_{13}| \leq (k/n^2) \sum_j \{x_j f(y+\theta_j)\psi'[2F(y) - 1 + \theta_j]\}^2$$
$$\leq (k/n^2) \sum x_j^2 \qquad \text{by (5.9)},$$
$$|B_{14}| \leq |B_{11}| + |B_{12}| \to 0 \qquad \text{uniformly in } t,$$
$$|B_{15}| \leq |B_{11}| + |B_{13}| \to 0 \qquad \text{uniformly in } t, \text{ finally}$$
$$|B_{16}| \leq |B_{12}| + |B_{13}|.$$

We have therefore proved that

$$\sup_{|t| \leq k} [n^{\frac{1}{2}}\{T_1(Y) - T_1(Y^*)\}] \to 0 \quad \text{in } P_0\text{-probability},$$

and it follows from the contiguity of P_0 and P_n that

$$\sup_{|t| \leq k} -n^{\frac{1}{2}}[T_1(Y) - T_1(Y^*)]^2 \to 0 \quad \text{in } P_n\text{-probability},$$

and the theorem is proved.

9. Acknowledgment. I should like to thank Professor Erich L. Lehmann, not only for suggesting this problem but also for his continued guidance and encouragement. I am also grateful to Professor J. Hájek for many helpful discussions, and to a referee for useful suggestions.

REFERENCES

[1] ADICHIE, J. N. (1967). Asymptotic efficiency of a class of non-parametric tests for regression parameters. *Ann. Math. Statist.* **38** 884–893.

[2] BICKEL, P. J. (1964). On some alternative estimates for shift in the p-variate one same problem. *Ann. Math. Statist.* **35** 1079–1090.

[3] BICKEL, P. J. (1965). On some asymptotically non-parametric competitors of Hotelling's T^2. *Ann. Math. Statist.* **36** 160–173.

[4] CRAMÉR, H. (1945). *Mathematical Methods of Statistics*. Princeton Univ. Press.

[5] EICKER, F. (1963). Asymptotic normality and consistency of the least squares estimators for families of linear regressions. *Ann. Math. Statist.* **34** 447–456.

[6] HÁJEK, J. (1962). Asymptotically most powerful rank order tests. *Ann. Math. Statist.* **33** 1124–1147.

[7] HEMELRIJK, J. (1949). Construction of a confidence region for a line. *Indag. Mth.* **11** 374–384.

[8] HILL, B. M. (1962). A test of linearity versus convexity of a median regression curve. *Ann. Math. Statist.* **33** 1096–1123.

[9] HODGES, J. L., JR. and LEHMANN, E. L. (1963). Estimates of location based on rank tests. *Ann. Math. Statist.* **34** 598–611.

[10] HOYLAND, A. (1965). Robustness of Hodges and Lehmann estimates for shift. *Ann. Math. Statist.* **36** 174–197.

[11] MOOD, A. M. (1950). *Introduction to the Theory of Statistics*. McGraw-Hill, New York.

[12] NAIR, K. R. and SHRIVASTAVA, M. D. (1942). On a simple method of curve fitting. *Sankhya* **6** 121–132.

[13] THEIL, H. (1950). A rank invariant method of linear and polynomial regression analysis. *Indag. Math.* **12** *Fasc.* **2** 85–91, 173–177.

[14] WALD, A. (1940). The fitting of straight lines if both variables are subject to error. *Ann. Math. Statist.* **11** 284–300.

This article was written in 1967

RANK SCORE COMPARISON OF SEVERAL REGRESSION PARAMETERS

BY J. N. ADICHIE

University of Nigeria, Nsukka

For testing $\beta_i = \beta$, $i = 1, \cdots, k$, in the model $Y_{ij} = \alpha + \beta_i x_{ij} + Z_{ij}$ $j = 1, \cdots, n_i$ a class of rank score tests is presented. The test statistic is based on the simultaneous ranking of all the observations in the different k samples. Its asymptotic distribution is proved to be chi square under the hypothesis and noncentral chi square under an appropriate sequence of alternatives. The asymptotic efficiency of the given procedure relative to the least squares procedure is shown to be the same as the efficiency of rank score tests relative to the t-test in the two sample problem. The proposed criterion would be an asymptotically most powerful rank score test for the hypothesis if the distribution function of the observations is known.

0. Introduction and summary. For the regression model $Y_{ij} = \alpha_i + \beta_i x_{ij} + Z_{ij}$, $j = 1, \cdots, n_i$; $i = 1, \cdots, k$ where Z_{ij} are independent random variables, a rank score method of testing that $\beta_i = \beta$ for all i, while α_i are nuisance parameters, was recently studied by Sen (1969). His test criteria are based on the individual ranks of the k different samples. In this paper, we show that for the special case where $\alpha_i = \alpha$ (unknown), suitable rank score tests for $\beta_i = \beta$ may be based on the simultaneous ranking of all the observations.

1. Notations and preliminaries. For each $i = 1, \cdots, k$, let Y_{ij}, $j = 1, \cdots, n_i$ be independent random variables with continuous distribution functions F_{ij} given by

$$P(Y_{ij} \leqq y) = F_{ij}(y) = F(y - \alpha - \beta_i x_{ij}) . \tag{1.1}$$

The precise functional form of $F(\cdot)$ is not assumed to be known. Here x_{ij}'s are known regression constants, α is a nuisance parameter and the β_i's are the quantities of interest. Our problem is to test the hypothesis

$$H_0 : \beta_i = \beta \quad \text{(unknown)} \tag{1.2}$$

against the set of alternatives that $\beta_1, \cdots, \beta_k$ are not all equal.

To simplify the notation, let us write

$$x_{i\cdot} = n_i^{-1} \sum_j x_{ij} ; \qquad C_{ni}^2 = \sum_j (x_{ij} - x_{i\cdot})^2 ; \qquad \gamma_{ni} = \{C_{ni}/C_n\}^2 \qquad i = 1, \cdots, k \tag{1.3}$$

$$C_n^2 = \sum_i C_{ni}^2 ; \qquad n = \sum_i n_i \tag{1.4}$$

where for the summations above, and in fact throughout the rest of the paper,

Received October 1972; revised March 1973.

AMS 1970 *subject classifications.* Primary 62G10, 62G20; Secondary 62E20, 62J05.

Key words and phrases. Simultaneous ranking, score generating function, bounded in probability, orthogonal transformation, asymptotic normality, asymptotic efficiency.

j goes from 1 to n_i; i (or s) goes from 1 to k. We shall also write

$$(1.5)\qquad c_{sj}^{(i)} = \gamma_{ni}(x_{sj} - x_{s\bullet}) \qquad s = 1, \cdots, i-1, i+1, \cdots, k$$
$$= (\gamma_{ni} - 1)(x_{sj} - x_{s\bullet}) \qquad s = i$$

so that

$$(1.6)\qquad \bar{c}^{(i)} = n^{-1} \textstyle\sum_s \sum_j c_{sj}^{(i)} = 0 \qquad i = 1, \cdots, k$$

and

$$(1.7)\qquad \textstyle\sum_s \sum_j \{c_{sj}^{(i)} - \bar{c}^{(i)}\}^2 = (\gamma_{ni} - \gamma_{ni}^2)C_n^{\,2} \leqq C_n^{\,2}\,.$$

It is assumed that each of the C_{ni}^2 (and hence $C_n^{\,2}$) tends to infinity with n such that

$$(1.8)\qquad \lim \gamma_{ni} = \gamma_i\,; \qquad 0 < \gamma_0 \leqq \gamma_1, \cdots, \gamma_k \leqq (1 - \gamma_0) < 1$$

where $\gamma_0 < 1/k$.

Let $\psi(u)$, $0 < u < 1$, be a smooth non-decreasing function, and let the scores generated by ψ be defined by

$$(1.9)\qquad a_n(p) = \psi\{p/(n+1)\} \qquad p = 1, \cdots, n\,.$$

Also let R_{ij} be the rank of Y_{ij} in the combined ranking of all the n observations. We shall need an estimate of β in (1.2); for that purpose, let

$$(1.10)\qquad S_n(Y) = \textstyle\sum_i \sum_j (x_{ij} - x_{i\bullet})a_n(R_{ij})\,.$$

As in Adichie (1967), define the estimate of β based on (1.10) as follows;

$$(1.11)\qquad \beta_n^{\,*} = \sup\{b : S_n(Y - bx) > 0\}\,; \qquad \beta_n^{\,**} = \inf\{b : S_n(Y - bx) < 0\}$$

$$(1.12)\qquad \hat{\beta}_n = \tfrac{1}{2}(\beta_n^{\,*} + \beta_n^{\,**})$$

where $S_n(Y - bx)$ denotes the statistic (1.10) when the observations Y_{ij} are replaced by $(Y_{ij} - bx_{ij})$. The estimate defined in (1.12) is consistent in the sense to be made precise in Lemma 2.1 below. Now write $\hat{Y}_{ij} = (Y_{ij} - \hat{\beta}x_{ij})$, and let $\hat{R}_{ij}$ be the ranks of $\hat{Y}_{ij}$. Define

$$(1.13)\qquad \hat{T}_{ni} = T_{ni}(\hat{Y}) = \textstyle\sum_s \sum_j c_{sj}^{(i)} a_n(\hat{R}_{sj})\,;$$

the proposed test statistic is

$$(1.14)\qquad \hat{L}_n = \textstyle\sum_i (\hat{T}_{ni}/AC_{ni})^2$$

where

$$(1.15)\qquad A^2 = \int \psi^2(u)\,du - \{\int \psi(u)\,du\}^2\,.$$

2. Asymptotic distribution of $\hat{L}_n$. In order to study the asymptotic power properties of the proposed $\hat{L}_n$ test, we shall establish the limiting distribution not only under the hypothesis H_0 but also under the sequence of alternatives,

$$(2.1)\qquad H_n : \beta_{ni} = \beta + (\theta_i/C_n)\,, \qquad |\theta_i| \leqq M_2\,, \qquad i = 1, \cdots, k\,.$$

Now set $Y_{ij}^0 = (Y_{ij} - \beta x_{ij})$, and let R_{ij}^0 be the ranks of Y_{ij}^0. Also let T_{ni}^0 and $L_n^{\,0}$

be the T_{ni}- and L_n-statistics associated with Y^0_{ij}. The proof of the limiting distribution of $\hat{L}_n$ depends on the following lemmas.

LEMMA 2.1. *Let $\hat{\beta}_n$ be as defined in* (1.12). *Assume that the score generating function $\phi(u)$, and the regression constants x_{ij} satisfy conditions* (i), (iii) *and* (iv) *of Lemma 2.2 below. Then as $n \to \infty$,*

(2.2) $\quad |C_n(\hat{\beta}_n - \beta)|$ *is bounded in both P_0 and P_n probabilities,*

where P_0 and P_n denote probabilities under (1.2) *and* (2.1) *respectively.*

PROOF. The proof of boundedness of (2.2) under P_n is similar to that of Lemma 3.1 of Sen (1969).

LEMMA 2.2. *Let the score generating function $\phi(u)$, $0 < u < 1$ have*

(i) *a bounded second derivative,*
(ii) $\sup_y [(d/dy)\phi\{F(y)\}]$ *also bounded; and let the regression constants be such that*
(iii) $\max_{ij} |x_{ij}| \leq M \max_{ij} |x_{ij} - x_{i\cdot}|$, *$M$ does not depend on n,*
(iv) $\{\max_{ij} (x_{ij} - x_{i\cdot})^2/C_n^2\} \to 0$.

Then for each i, $\{\hat{T}_{ni} - T^0_{ni})/C_n\} \to 0$ in both P_0- and P_n-probabilities.

PROOF. Without loss of generality, we may take $\alpha = \beta = 0$. Throughout the proof, M will denote a generic constant independent of n. Now let us write

(2.3) $$Y^*_{ij} = Y_{ij} - (b/C_n)x_{ij}\,, \qquad |b| \leq M$$

and let $T^*_{ni} = T_{ni}(Y^*)$ be the T_{ni}-statistic defined through Y^*_{ij}'s. To prove the lemma, under H_n, it is sufficient because of Lemma 2.1, to show that as $n \to \infty$,

(2.4) $$E_n\{(T^*_{ni} - T^0_{ni})/C_n\}^2 \to 0 \qquad \text{uniformly in } |b| \leq M\,,$$

where E_n denotes expectation taken under H_n of (2.1). Repeated use will be made of the fact that under H_n, with $\alpha = \beta = 0$, the distribution functions of Y^0_{ij} and Y^*_{ij} are respectively,

(2.5) $$F^0_{ij}(y) = F\{y - (bx_{ij}/C_n)\}\,; \qquad F^*_{ij}(y) = F\{y - (\theta_i - b)x_{ij}/C_n\}\,.$$

Following Hájek (1968) define, for each i, a sum of n independent random variables with zero expectation; thus

(2.6) $$Z_{ni} = Z_{ni}(Y) = \textstyle\sum_s \sum_j n^{-1} \sum_t \sum_v (c^{(i)}_{tv} - c^{(i)}_{sj})B_{tv}(Y_{sj})$$

where

(2.7) $$-B_{tv}(Y_{sj}) = \phi\{F_{sj}(Y_{sj})\} + Q_{sjtv}(Y_{sj}) + \text{const.}\,,$$

and

(2.8) $$|Q_{sjtv}(y)| \leq M \max_{sjt,v,y} |F_{sj}(y) - F_{tv}(y)|\,.$$

Also for each i, set

(2.9) $$\mu_{ni} = \textstyle\sum_s \sum_j c^{(i)}_{sj} \int \phi\{\bar{F}(y)\}\, dF_{sj}(y)$$

where

$$n\bar{F}(y) = \sum_s \sum_j F_{sj}(y)\,. \tag{2.10}$$

Correspondingly, let Z^*_{ni} and μ^*_{ni} be the statistic (2.6) and the quantity (2.9) defined through Y^*_{ij}'s. On writing

$$\begin{aligned} E_n(T^*_{ni} - T^0_{ni})^2 = E_n\{(T^*_{ni} - Z^*_{ni} - \mu^*_{ni}) - (T^0_{ni} - Z^0_{ni} - \mu^0_{ni}) \\ - (Z^0_{ni} - Z^*_{ni} - \mu^*_{ni} + \mu^0_{ni})\}^2 \end{aligned} \tag{2.11}$$

and making repeated use of the elementary inequality $(b - d)^2 \leqq 2(b^2 + d^2)$ we obtain

$$\begin{aligned} E_n(T^*_{ni} - T^0_{ni})^2 \leqq 4E_n(T^*_{ni} - Z^*_{ni} - \mu^*_{ni})^2 + 4E_n(T^0_{ni} - Z^0_{ni} - \mu^0_{ni})^2 \\ + 2E_n(Z^0_{ni} - Z^*_{ni})^2 + 2(\mu^0_{ni} - \mu^*_{ni})^2\,. \end{aligned} \tag{2.12}$$

For the first two terms of the inequality, Hájek (1968) has shown that under our condition (i) alone, and in view of (1.6)

$$\begin{aligned} &E_n(T_{ni} - Z_{ni} - \mu_{ni})^2 \\ &\leqq M_1 n^{-1} \sum_s \sum_j \{c^{(i)}_{sj}\}^2 \\ &\leqq M_1 \max_{sj} (c^{(i)}_{sj})^2 \\ &= M_1 \max\{\gamma^{-2}_{ni} \max_{t\neq i,j} (x_{tj} - x_{t\bullet})^2, (1 - \gamma_{ni})^2 \max_j (x_{ij} - x_{i\bullet})^2\} \\ &\leqq M_1 \max_{sj} (x_{sj} - x_{s\bullet})^2\,. \end{aligned} \tag{2.13}$$

As for the term $E_n(Z^0_{ni} - Z^*_{ni})^2$, (2.6), (2.7) and (2.8) imply that

$$\begin{aligned} |Z^0_{ni}(y) - Z^*_{ni}(y)| \leqq \sum_s \sum_j n^{-1} \sum_t \sum_v |c^{(i)}_{tv} - c^{(i)}_{sj}| \\ \times |\psi\{F^*_{sj}(y)\} - \psi\{F^0_{sj}(y)\}| + |Q_{sjtv}(y) - Q^*_{sjtv}(y)|\,. \end{aligned} \tag{2.14}$$

Furthermore, by (2.5) and conditions (ii) and (iii) of the lemma, we have

$$\begin{aligned} |\psi\{F^*_{sj}(y)\} - \psi\{F^0_{sj}(y)\}| &\leqq \max_{sj} |x_{sj}|(\theta_s/C_n)\psi'\{F(y)\}f(y) \\ &\leqq M \max_{sj} |x_{sj}|/C_n \\ &\leqq M_1 \max_{sj} |x_{sj} - x_{s\bullet}|/C_n\,. \end{aligned} \tag{2.15}$$

Also (2.5), (2.8) and condition (iii) imply

$$\begin{aligned} &|Q^0_{sjtv}(y) - Q^*_{sjtv}(y)| \\ &\leqq \max_{sjtvy} [f(y)\{|x_{tv} - x_{sj}|(b/C_n) + |\theta_t x_{tv} - \theta_s x_{sj}|/C_n\}] \\ &\leqq M_2 \max_{sj} |x_{sj} - x_{s\bullet}|/C_n\,. \end{aligned} \tag{2.16}$$

On applying (2.15) and (2.16) in (2.14) and making use of the inequality

$$\sum_s \sum_j (n^{-1} \sum_t \sum_v |c^{(i)}_{tv} - c^{(i)}_{sj}|)^2 \leqq 2 \sum_s \sum_j \{c^{(i)}_{sj}\}^2 \leqq 2C_n^2 \tag{2.17}$$

it follows, since the Z_{ni}'s are sums of independent random variables with zero expectations, that

$$E_n(Z^0_{ni} - Z^*_{ni})^2 \leqq M \max_{sj} (x_{sj} - x_{s\bullet})^2\,. \tag{2.18}$$

Finally, we write

$$(\mu^0_{ni} - \mu^*_{ni}) = \sum_s \sum_j c^{(i)}_{sj}[\int \psi\{\bar{F}^0(y)\}\, dF^0_{sj}(y) - \int \psi\{\bar{F}^*(y)\}\, dF^*_{sj}(y)]\,.$$

On expanding and integrating by parts, making use of (2.5), the terms in the square brackets give

$$C_n^{-1}[-\theta_s x_{sj} \int \psi_y'\{F(y)\}\, dF(y) - bx_{..} \int \psi_y'\{F(y)\}F^0_{sj}(y)$$
$$+ n^{-1} \sum_s \sum_j (\theta_s - b)x_{sj} \int \psi_y'\{F(y)\}\, dF^*_{sj}(y)]\,,$$

where $x_{..} = n^{-1} \sum_i \sum_j x_{ij}$, and ψ_y' denotes the derivative of ψ with respect to y. In view of (2.1), and conditions (ii) and (iii) of the lemma,

$$|\mu^0_{ni} - \mu^*_{ni}| \leqq C_n^{-1}|M_2 M_3 x_{sj} + \{bM_4 + M_5(M_2 - b)\}x_{..}| \sum_s \sum_j |c^{(i)}_{sj}|$$
$$\leqq (M_6/C_n) \max_{sj} |x_{sj} - x_{s.}| \sum_s \sum_j |c^{(i)}_{sj}|\,,$$

where M with subscripts are also generic constants. It follows then from (1.7), that

$$(2.19) \qquad (\mu^0_{ni} - \mu^*_{ni})^2 \leqq M \max_{sj} (x_{sj} - x_{s.})^2\,.$$

The inequalities (2.13), (2.18) and (2.19) together imply (2.4) and the lemma is proved. The convergence of $E_0\{(T^*_{ni} - T^*_{ni})^2/C_n^2\}$ to zero follows as an obvious corollary.

LEMMA 2.3. *If* $\hat{U}_{ni} = (\hat{T}_{ni}/AC_{ni})$, *then under the conditions of Lemma 2.2, the random vector* $\hat{\mathbf{U}}_n' = (\hat{U}_{n1}, \cdots, \hat{U}_{nk})$ *is asymptotically normal* $N(\mathbf{0}, \Sigma)$ *under* P_0, *and* $N(\boldsymbol{\nu}_n, \Sigma)$ *under* P_n, *where* $\boldsymbol{\nu}_n' = (\nu_{n1}, \cdots, \nu_{nk})$, *with*

$$(2.20) \qquad \nu_{ni} = \gamma^{\frac{1}{2}}_{ni}\{\theta_i - \sum_s (\gamma_{ns}\theta_s)\} \int \psi_y'\{F(y)\}\, dF(y)/A$$

$$(2.21) \qquad \Sigma = (\sigma_{is})\,; \qquad \sigma_{is} = \{\delta_{is} - (\gamma_{ni}\gamma_{ns})^{\frac{1}{2}}\}$$

where δ *denotes the Kronecker delta.*

PROOF. The proof will be given only for P_n. By virtue of Lemma 2.2 $\{\hat{T}_{ni}/C_n\}$ and $\{T^0_{ni}/C_n\}$ have the same limiting distribution. Now, since under (2.1) with $\beta = 0$

$$\max_{sjtvy} |F_{sj}(y) - F_{tv}(y)| \leqq M \max_{sj} |x_{sj} - x_{s.}|/C_n$$

and

$$\max_{sj} [\{c^{(i)}_{sj}\}^2/\sum_s \sum_j \{c^{(i)}_{sj}\}^2] \leqq M_1 \max_{sj} (x_{sj} - x_{s.})^2/(\gamma_{ni} - \gamma^2_{ni})C_n^2$$
$$\leqq M \max_{sj} (x_{sj} - x_{s.})^2/C_n^2$$

it follows from Theorem 2.2 of Hájek (1968) that $(T^0_{ni} - \mu_{ni})/A(1 - \gamma_{ni})^{\frac{1}{2}}C_{ni}$, and hence $(\hat{T}_{ni} - \mu_{ni})/A(1 - \gamma_{ni})^{\frac{1}{2}}C_{ni}$ is asymptotically normal $N(0, 1)$.
But under (2.1),

$$(\mu_{ni}/AC_{ni}) = [\{\mu_{ni}(\beta_{ni}) - \mu_{ni}(0)\}/AC_{ni}] \sim \nu_{ni}$$

where $\mu_{ni}(\beta_{ni})$ and $\mu_{ni}(0)$ are the values of (2.9) computed under (2.1) and (1.2) respectively. Hence under (2.1),

$$(2.22) \qquad \hat{U}_{ni} \text{ is asymptotically } N(\nu_{ni}, 1 - \gamma_{ni}) \qquad i = 1, \cdots, k\,.$$

Furthermore, any linear combination of the $\hat{T}_{ni}$'s is of the form

$$\hat{T}_n = \sum_i \lambda_i T_{ni} = \sum_i \sum_s \sum_j \lambda_i c_{sj}^{(i)} a_n(\hat{R}_{sj}) .$$

It is easy to see that the new constants $(\lambda_i c_{sj}^{(i)})$ satisfy the Noether condition with $c_{sj}^{(i)}$, so that under the assumptions of Lemma 2.2 $\hat{T}_n$ has a limiting normal distribution under (2.1). Hence $\hat{\mathbf{U}}_n$ is asymptotically normal. Now if we write

$$W_{ni} = \sum_s \sum_j c_{sj}^{(i)} \psi\{F_{sj}(Y_{sj})\}/AC_{ni} , \qquad i = 1, \cdots, k$$

it can be shown by arguments similar to those used in the proof of Theorem 2.2 of Hájek (1968), that under (2.1),

(2.23) $$\mathrm{Cov}\,(U_{ni}^0, U_{ns}^0) \sim \mathrm{Cov}\,(W_{ni}, W_{ns}) = -(\gamma_{ni}\gamma_{ns})^{\frac{1}{2}} .$$

The symbol $\sim$ denotes asymptotic equivalence. In view of Lemma 2.2,

(2.24) $$\mathrm{Cov}\,(\hat{U}_{ni}, \hat{U}_{ns}) \sim -(\gamma_{ni}\gamma_{ns})^{\frac{1}{2}} .$$

The proof of the lemma is complete.
The main result of the paper is given in the following

THEOREM 2.1. *Consider model* (1.1) *and assume that the conditions of Lemma* 2.2 *are satisfied. Then*

(2.25) $$\lim P_0(\hat{L}_n \leqq y) = P(\chi_{k-1}^2 \leqq y)$$

(2.26) $$\lim P_n(\hat{L}_n \leqq y) = P(\chi_{k-1}^2(\Delta_L) \leqq y)$$

where $\chi_{k-1}^2(\Delta_L)$ *denotes the noncentral chi-square random variable with* $(k-1)$ *degrees of freedom and noncentrality parameter*

(2.27) $$\Delta_L = \sum_i \nu_{ni}^2 = \{\sum_i \gamma_{ni}\theta_i^2 - (\sum_i \gamma_{ni}\theta_i)^2\}[\int \psi_y'\{F(y)\}\, dF(y)]^2/A^2 .$$

PROOF. The asymptotic covariance matrix (2.21) of the vector $\hat{\mathbf{U}}_n$ is singular of rank $(k-1)$. On using an orthogonal transformation, e.g.

(2.28) $$V_0 = \sum_s \gamma_{ns}^{\frac{1}{2}} \hat{U}_{ns}$$
$$V_i = \sum_s e_{is} \hat{U}_{ns} \qquad i = 1, \cdots, (k-1)$$

where the e's are properly chosen to make the transformation orthogonal, it follows from Lemma 2.3 that under (1.2) the sum of squares $\hat{L}_n = \sum_i \hat{U}_{ni}^2$ has asymptotically a central chi-square distribution with $(k-1)$ degrees of freedom, and under (2.1) has asymptotically a noncentral chi-square distribution with $(k-1)$ degrees of freedom, and noncentrality parameter $\sum_i \nu_{ni}^2$ given in (2.27).

In view of (2.25) an asymptotically level ε test rejects the hypothesis (1.2) if $\hat{L}_n$ is greater than the upper $100\varepsilon\%$ point of the chi-square distribution with $(k-1)$ degrees of freedom.

3. Asymptotic efficiency. The usual method of testing the hypothesis (1.2) in the model (1.1) is based on the least squares estimates $\tilde{\beta}_n$ and $\tilde{\beta}_{ni}$ of the parameters β and β_i. In computing the estimates, it is easier to work with $x_{ij}' = (x_{ij} - x_{i\cdot})$ instead of the original x_{ij}. With this reparametrization, the test statistic becomes

$$M_n = \sum_i C_{ni}^2(\hat{\beta}_{ni} - \hat{\beta}_n)^2/(k-1)s_e^2 \tag{3.1}$$

where

$$\hat{\beta}_{ni} = \sum_j Y_{ij}(x_{ij} - x_{i\cdot})/C_{ni}^2\,; \qquad \hat{\beta}_n = \sum_i \gamma_{ni}\hat{\beta}_{ni}\,, \tag{3.2}$$

and s_e^2 is the mean square due to error. It is well known that for any distribution function $F(y)$ for which $\sigma^2(F) = \{\int y^2\, dF(y) - (\int y\, dF(y))^2\} < \infty$,

$$\lim P_0\{(k-1)M_n \leq y\} = P(\chi_{k-1}^2 \leq y) \tag{3.3}$$

$$\lim P_n\{(k-1)M_n \leq y\} = P\{\chi_{k-1}^2(\Delta_M) \leq y\} \tag{3.4}$$

where

$$\Delta_M = \{\sum_i \gamma_{ni}\theta_i^2 - (\sum_i \gamma_{ni}\theta_i)^2\}/\sigma^2(F)\,. \tag{3.5}$$

By the conventional method of measuring asymptotic efficiency, the efficiency of $\hat{L}_n$ test relative to the usual least squares test is therefore

$$\Delta_L/\Delta_M = \sigma^2(F)[\int \psi_y'\{F(y)\}\, dF(y)]^2/A^2\,. \tag{3.6}$$

The efficiency in (3.6) is the same as that obtained by Sen, and it is the familiar efficiency of rank tests relative to the classical tests. The connection between efficiency and asymptotic power of tests is now well established (see e.g. Theorem 6.1 of Hájek (1962)). If the functional form of the distribution function F is known, one can improve on both the classical and the rank score tests. Provided F has a finite Fisher information, an asymptotically optimum parametric test is not M_n, but the likelihood ratio test (see Section 2 of Sen (1969) for details). For the rank score tests, if we choose the score generating function

$$\psi(u) = -[f'\{F^{-1}(u)\}/f\{F^{-1}(u)\}]\,, \tag{3.7}$$

it follows that under the assumptions of Lemma 2.2 our $\hat{L}_n$ test based on (3.7), with $\int \psi^2(u)\, du < \infty$, provides an asymptotically most powerful rank order test for the hypothesis (1.2) in model (1.1).

REFERENCES

[1] ADICHIE, J. N. (1967). Estimates of ergression parameters based on rank tests. *Ann. Math. Statist.* **38** 894–904.

[2] HÁJEK, J. (1962). Asymptotically most powerful rank order tests. *Ann. Math. Statist.* **33** 1124–1147.

[3] HÁJEK, J. (1968). Asymptotic normality of simple linear rank statistics under alternatives. *Ann. Math. Statist.* **39** 325–346.

[4] SEN, P. K. (1969). On a class of rank order tests for the parallelism of several regression lines. *Ann. Math. Statist.* **40** 1668–1683.

DEPARTMENT OF MATHEMATICS AND STATISTICS
UNIVERSITY OF NIGERIA
NSUKKA
EAST CENTRAL STATE, NIGERIA

ON THE USE OF RANKS FOR TESTING THE COINCIDENCE OF SEVERAL REGRESSION LINES

BY J. N. ADICHIE

University of Nigeria, Nsukka

For several linear regression lines $Y_{ij} = \alpha_i + \beta_i(x_{ij} - x_{i.}) + Z_{ij}$, $i = 1, \cdots, k$; $j = 1, \cdots, n_i$, a statistic for testing $\alpha_i = \alpha$, $\beta_i = \beta$ is constructed based on the simultaneous ranking of all the observations. The asymptotic properties of the criterion are also studied. The results are, however, not directly applicable to the general design model $Y_{ij} = \alpha_i + \beta_i x_{ij} + Z_{ij}$, unless it is assumed that the group means $x_{i.}$ are all equal.

0. Introduction and summary. In two recent papers Sen (1969, 1972) considered several regression lines $Y_{ij} = \alpha_i + \beta_i x_{ij} + Z_{ij}$, $i = 1, \cdots, k$; $j = 1, \cdots, n_i$, and studied optimum rank score tests for the separate hypotheses H_1: $\beta_i = \beta$ (unknown), α_i are nuisance parameters and H_2: $\alpha_i = \alpha$ (unknown), β_i are nuisance parameters. In the present paper, we propose rank score tests that discriminate simultaneously against different β's and different α's. The methods of Sen could be used to construct rank order statistics for testing H_0: $\alpha_i = \alpha$, $\beta_i = \beta$. This would, however, involve the estimation of α and the β_i and the combination of the separate k rankings. The alternative method presented below makes use of the simultaneous ranking of all the observations, and involves the estimation of β only. However, our procedure is limited to designs where the group means $x_{i.}$ of x_{ij}'s are all equal.

The proposed test statistic is shown to have a limiting chi-square distribution under the hypothesis and a non-central chi-square under an appropriate sequence of alternatives. The asymptotic efficiency of the given procedure relative to the least squares procedure is also shown to be the familiar efficiency of rank score tests relative to the t-test in the two-sample problem.

1. Notation and assumptions. For each $i = 1, \cdots, k$, let Y_{ij}, $j = 1, \cdots, n_i$; be independent random variables. Also let x_{ij} be known constants that are not all equal. It is assumed that the distribution function $F_{ij}(\cdot)$ of Y_{ij} are given by

$$(1.1) \qquad P(Y_{ij} < y) = F_{ij}(y) = F\{y - \alpha_i - \beta_i(x_{ij} - x_{i.})\}$$

where $x_{i.} = n_i^{-1} \sum_j x_{ij}$, F is continuous but its functional form need not be known, and α_i, β_i are the unknown parameters of interest. Our problem is to test the hypothesis

$$(1.2) \qquad H_0: \alpha_i = \alpha \quad \text{(unknown)}, \qquad \beta_i = \beta \quad \text{(unknown)},$$

against the set of alternatives that violate (1.2).

Received November 1972; revised January 1974.

AMS 1970 *subject classifications.* Primary 62G10, 62G20; Secondary 62E20, 62J05.

Key words and phrases. Linear rank statistic, score generating function, bounded in probability, least squares estimates, asymptotic efficiency.

REMARK. The model in (1.1) assumes that the x_{ij}'s have been centered about their group means $x_{i.}$. This assumption, which necessarily limits the scope of our procedure to specially balanced designs, is equivalent to the so-called "orthogonality condition" in the classical least squares regression theory. For testing hypothesis about β_i, test criteria are always available independent of α_i, and without extra condition on the distribution functions F_{ij}. On the other hand, tests about α_i usually depend on the β_i and require some symmetry condition. The symmetry effect may be achieved if either the F_{ij} are symmetric or the x_{ij} are symmetrically balanced as in (1.1) (see e.g., Hájek (1969), Theorem 3F).

In order to maintain the notation in Adichie (1974), we shall actually be considering sequences $\{Y_{nij}\}$ and $\{x_{nij}\}$, $n = 1, 2, \cdots$, of independent random variables, and constants respectively. However, for simplicity of notation, the dependence on n of Y_{ij}, x_{ij} and some of their function, will often be suppressed. We shall therefore write

$$(1.3)\qquad C_{ni}^2 = \sum_j (x_{ij} - x_{i.})^2\,, \qquad \gamma_{ni} = C_{ni}^2/C_n^2\,,$$
$$\lambda_{ni} = (n_i/n)\,, \qquad \rho_{ni} = (n_i/C_n)\,, \qquad i = 1, \cdots, k\,,$$

where

$$(1.4)\qquad C_n^2 = \sum_i C_{ni}^2\,; \qquad n = \sum_i n_i\,.$$

For all the summations in this paper, i, s, and t go from 1 to k, while j or v goes from 1 to n_i or n_t. All limits are taken as $n \to \infty$. It is assumed that each of the quantities n_i and C_{ni}^2 increases with n in such a way that for each $i = 1, \cdots, k$,

$$(1.5)\qquad \begin{aligned} &0 < \gamma_0 < (\sup_n \gamma_{ni}) < (1 - \gamma_0) < 1\,,\\ &0 < \lambda_0 \leqq (\sup_n \lambda_{ni}) \leqq (1 - \lambda_0) < 1\,,\\ &0 < \rho_0 \leqq (\sup_n \rho_{ni}) < K\,,\end{aligned}$$

and $\max(\gamma_0, \lambda_0) < (1/k)$. Throughout this paper K with or without subscripts will denote a generic constant. We shall write

$$(1.6)\qquad \begin{aligned} c_{sj}^{(i)} &= \gamma_{ni}(x_{sj} - x_{s.}) && s\,(\neq i) = 1, \cdots, k\,,\\ &= -(1 - \gamma_{ni})(x_{sj} - x_{s.}) && s = i\,,\end{aligned}$$

$$(1.7)\qquad \begin{aligned} d_{sj}^{(i)} &= 0 && s \neq i\,,\\ &= 1 && s = i\,,\end{aligned}$$

so that

$$(1.8)\qquad \bar{d}^{(i)} = n^{-1} \sum_s \sum_j d_{sj}^{(i)} = \lambda_{ni}\,; \qquad \bar{c}^{(i)} = 0\,,$$

$$(1.9)\qquad \sum_s \sum_j (d_{sj}^{(i)} - \bar{d}^{(i)})^2 = \rho_{ni}(1 - \lambda_{ni})C_n^2\,,$$

and

$$(1.10)\qquad \sum_s \sum_j (c_{sj}^{(i)} - \bar{c}^{(i)})^2 = \gamma_{ni}(1 - \gamma_{ni})C_n^2\,.$$

2. The test statistic. Let $\psi(u)$, $0 < u < 1$, be a smooth non-decreasing function, and let the scores generated by ψ be defined by

$$(2.1) \qquad a_n(p) = \psi\{p/(n+1)\}, \qquad p = 1, \cdots, n.$$

Also let R_{ij} be the rank of Y_{ij} in the combined ranking of all the n observations. For the unknown β in (1.2), we shall require an estimate $\hat{\beta}$ defined in Adichie (1974). For ease of reference, the estimate is

$$(2.2) \qquad \hat{\beta} = \tfrac{1}{2}(\beta_n{}^* + \beta_n{}^{**}),$$

where

$$(2.3) \qquad \beta_n{}^* = \sup\{b : S_n(Y - bx) > 0\}, \qquad \beta_n{}^{**} = \inf\{b : S_n(Y - bx) < 0\},$$

and $S_n(Y - bx)$ denotes the statistic

$$(2.4) \qquad S_n(Y) = \textstyle\sum_i \sum_j (x_{ij} - x_{i.})a_n(R_{ij}),$$

when the observations Y_{ij} are replaced by $\{Y_{ij} - b(x_{ij} - x_{i.})\}$.

Now write $\hat{Y}_{ij} = \{Y_{ij} - \hat{\beta}(x_{ij} - x_{i.})\}$, and let $\hat{R}_{ij}$ be the rank of $\hat{Y}_{ij}$. For each $i = 1, \cdots, k$, define

$$(2.5) \qquad \hat{T}_{\alpha ni} = \textstyle\sum_s \sum_j (d_{sj}^{(i)} - \bar{d}^{(i)})a_n(\hat{R}_{sj}),$$

$$(2.6) \qquad \hat{T}_{\beta ni} = \textstyle\sum_s \sum_j c_{sj}^{(i)} a_n(\hat{R}_{sj}).$$

Also for each i, let

$$(2.7) \qquad \hat{V}_{ni} = n^{-\frac{1}{2}}(\hat{T}_{\alpha ni}/A); \qquad \hat{U}_{ni} = (\hat{T}_{\beta ni}/AC_{ni}),$$

where

$$(2.8) \qquad A^2 = \textstyle\int \psi^2(u)\,du - \{\int \psi(u)\,du\}^2.$$

The proposed test statistic is

$$(2.9) \qquad M_n = \textstyle\sum_i (\hat{V}_{ni}^2 + \hat{U}_{ni}^2).$$

3. Asymptotic distribution of $\hat{M}_n$. We shall consider the limiting distribution, not only under the hypothesis (1.2), but also under a sequence of alternatives defined by

$$(3.1) \qquad H_n : \alpha_i = \alpha + (\xi_i/C_n); \qquad \beta_i = \beta + (\theta_i/C_n),$$

where $|\xi_i| < K_2$ and $|\theta_i| < K_3$, $i = 1, \cdots, k$.

Now set $Y_{ij}^0 = \{Y_{ij} - \beta(x_{ij} - x_{i.})\}$, and let R_{ij}^0 be the rank of Y_{ij}^0. For the proof of the limiting distribution we shall need the following $2k$ statistics:

$$(3.2) \qquad T_{\alpha ni}^0 = \textstyle\sum_s \sum_j \{d_{sj}^{(i)} - \bar{d}^{(i)}\}a_n(R_{sj}^0),$$

$$(3.3) \qquad T_{\beta ni}^0 = \textstyle\sum_s \sum_j c_{sj}^{(i)} a_n(R_{sj}^0), \qquad i = 1, \cdots, k.$$

Observe that, although neither (3.2) nor (3.3) can be calculated, because they depend on the unobservable random variables Y_{ij}^0 their distributions are fairly well known both under H_0 and H_n. The main tool in the proof of the limiting distribution of $\hat{M}_n$ is the following lemma

LEMMA 3.1. *Let the score generating function* $\psi(u)$ $0 < u < 1$, *satisfy the following*

(i) $|\psi''(u)| < K_4$,
(ii) $\sup_y |\psi_y'\{F(y)\}| < K_5$.

Also let the regression constants be such that

(iii) $\{\max_{ij} |x_{ij} - x_{i.}|/C_n\} \to 0$,

and assume that the estimate $\hat{\beta}$ *defined in* (2.2) *is such that as* $n \to \infty$,

(iv) $|C_n(\hat{\beta} - \beta)|$ *is bounded in both* P_0 *and* P_n *probabilities. Then under* (1.5), *for each* $1 = 1, \cdots, k$,

$$\{(\hat{T}_{\alpha ni} - T^0_{\alpha ni})/C_n\} \to 0 \,, \tag{3.4}$$

$$\{\hat{T}^0_{\beta ni} - T^0_{\beta ni})/C_n\} \to 0 \,, \tag{3.5}$$

in both P_0 *and* P_n *probabilities, where* ψ' *denotes the derivative, and* ψ_y' *the derivative with respect to* y, *while* P_0 *and* P_n *denote probabilities under* (1.2) *and* (3.1) *respectively.*

PROOF. The detailed proof of (3.5), under a slightly different P_n has been given in Adichie (1974). The proof of (3.4) proceeds on similar lines, upon defining Hájek's projection statistics for T^0_{ni}, and noting that in view of (1.7), (1.8) and (1.9), the constants $d^{(i)}_{sj}$ satisfy condition (iii) of the lemma. The proof that $\hat{\beta}$-estimate satisfies condition (iv) of the lemma is similar to that given in Sen (1969).

LEMMA 3.2. *Let* $\hat{V}_{ni}$ *and* $\hat{U}_{ni}$ *be as defined in* (2.7), *and let*

$$\mu_{\alpha ni} = \textstyle\sum_s \sum_j (d^{(i)}_{sj} - \bar{d}^{(i)}) \int \psi\{\bar{F}(y)\}\, dF_{sj}(y) \,, \tag{3.6}$$

$$\mu_{\beta ni} = \textstyle\sum_s \sum_j c^{(i)}_{sj} \int \psi\{\bar{F}(y)\}\, dF_{sj}(y) \,, \tag{3.7}$$

where

$$\bar{F}(y) = n^{-1} \textstyle\sum_s \sum_j F_{sj}(y) \,. \tag{3.8}$$

Then, under the conditions of Lemma 3.1

(i) $\hat{\mathbf{V}}_n' = (\hat{V}_{n1}, \cdots, \hat{V}_{nk})$ *is asymptotically* $N(\mathbf{0}, \Sigma_\alpha)$ *under* P_0, *and asymptotically* $N(\boldsymbol{\nu}_{\alpha n}, \Sigma_\alpha)$ *under* P_n;
(ii) $\hat{\mathbf{U}}_n' = (\hat{U}_{n1}, \cdots, \hat{U}_{nk})$ *is asymptotically* $N(\mathbf{0}, \Sigma_\beta)$ *under* P_0, *and asymptotically* $N(\boldsymbol{\nu}_{\beta n}, \Sigma_\beta)$ *under* P_n;
(iii) $\hat{\mathbf{V}}_n$ *and* $\hat{\mathbf{U}}_n$ *are asymptotically independent both under* P_0 *and* P_n;

where $\boldsymbol{\nu}'_{\alpha n} = (\nu_{\alpha n1}, \cdots, \nu_{\alpha nk})$, $\boldsymbol{\nu}'_{\beta n} = (\nu_{\beta n1}, \cdots, \nu_{\beta nk})$, *with*

$$\nu_{\alpha ni} = n^{-\frac{1}{2}}(\mu_{\alpha ni}/A) \,, \qquad \nu_{\beta ni} = (\mu_{\beta ni}/AC_{ni}) \,; \tag{3.9}$$

$$\Sigma_\alpha = (\sigma_{\alpha is}) \,; \qquad \sigma_{\alpha is} = \{\delta_{is} - (\lambda_{ni}\lambda_{ns})^{\frac{1}{2}}\} \,, \tag{3.10}$$

$$\Sigma_\beta = (\sigma_{\beta is}) \,; \qquad \sigma_{\beta is} = \{\delta_{is} - (\gamma_{ni}\gamma_{ns})^{\frac{1}{2}}\} \,, \tag{3.11}$$

and δ_{is} *is the Kronecker delta.*

PROOF. If the lemma is true for P_n then it is a fortiori true for P_0, so the proof is given for P_n. Without loss of generality, we take $\alpha = \beta = 0$, and by Lemma 3.1, we restrict attention to $\mathbf{V}_n{}^0$ and $\mathbf{U}_n{}^0$ defined through $T^0_{\alpha ni}$ and $T^0_{\beta ni}$. Now under (3.1) with $\alpha = \beta = 0$,

$$F^0_{ij}(y) = F\{y - (\xi_i/C_n) - (\theta_i/C_n)(x_{ij} - x_{i.})\},$$

so that

$$\begin{aligned}\max_{sjtvy} |F_{sj}(y) - F_{tv}(y)| &\leq K_7|(\xi_t - \xi_s) + \theta_t(x_{tv} - x_{t.}) - \theta_s(x_{sj} - x_{s.})|/C_n \\ &\leq 2K_7(K_5 + K_6)\max_{sj}|x_{sj} - x_{s.}|/C_n \\ &\leq K\max_{sj}|x_{sj} - x_{s.}|/C_n .\end{aligned}$$

Also because of (1.5), (1.7), (1.8) and (1.9),

$$\begin{aligned}&\max_{sj}|d^{(i)}_{sj} - \bar{d}^{(i)}|/\{\textstyle\sum_s \sum_j (d^{(i)}_{sj} - \bar{d}^{(i)})^2\}^{\frac{1}{2}} \\ &\qquad = \max\{\lambda_{ni.}(1 - \lambda_{ni})\}/\{\rho_{ni}(1 - \lambda_{ni})\}^{\frac{1}{2}}C_n \\ &\qquad \leq \{(\rho_0\lambda_0)^{-\frac{1}{2}}/C_n\} \leq K_0\max_{sj}|x_{sj} - x_{s.}|/C_n .\end{aligned}$$

for some appropriate K_0. It follows then from Theorem 2.2 of Hájek (1968), tnat under (2.1), $n_i^{-\frac{1}{2}}(T^0_{\alpha ni} - \mu_{\alpha ni})/A(1 - \lambda_{ni})^{\frac{1}{2}}$ is asymptotically $N(0, 1)$. Furthermore, any linear combination of the k statistics $T^0_{\alpha ni}$ is again a linear rank statistic whose constants satisfy condition (iii) of Lemma 3.1. Hence $\mathbf{V}_n{}^0$ under P_n is asymptotically normal with asymptotic mean $\boldsymbol{\nu}_{\alpha n}$. For the asymptotic covariance matrix, if we write

$$W_{\alpha ni} = n^{-\frac{1}{2}}\textstyle\sum_s \sum_j (d^{(i)}_{sj} - \bar{d}^{(i)})\phi\{F_{sj}(y)\}/A ,$$

then arguments similar to those used in the proof of Theorem 2.2 of Hájek (1968) show that under (3.1),

$$\text{Cov}(V^0_{ni}, V^0_{ns}) \sim \text{Cov}(W_{\alpha ni}, W_{\alpha ns}) = -(\lambda_{ni}\lambda_{ns})^{\frac{1}{2}} ,$$

where $\sim$ denotes asymptotic equivalence in the ratio sense. This establishes (i) of the lemma. The proof for (ii) is similar. Finally (iii) follows from the fact that

$$\textstyle\sum_s \sum_j c^{(i)}_{sj}(d^{(i)}_{sj} - \bar{d}^{(i)}) = 0 .$$

The limiting distribution of $\hat{M}$ is given in the following

THEOREM 3.1. *Consider model* (1.1), *and assume that the conditions of Lemma* 3.1 *are satisfied. Then under* P_0, $\hat{M}_n$ *has asymptotically a chi-square distribution with* $2k - 2$ *degrees of freedom, and under* P_n, *a non-central chi-square distribution with* $2k - 2$ *degrees of freedom and non-centrality parameter given by*

$$\Delta_M = \textstyle\sum_i\{\rho_i(\xi_i - \bar{\xi})^2 + \gamma_i(\theta_i - \bar{\theta})^2\}[\int \phi_v{}^2(F(y)\,dF(y))/A]^2 , \tag{3.12}$$

where $\bar{\xi} = \sum_i \lambda_i\xi_i$; $\bar{\theta} = \sum_i \gamma_i\theta_i$, *and* ρ_i, λ_i *are the limits of* ρ_{ni} *and* λ_{ni} *respectively.*

PROOF. Each of the covariance matrices (3.10) and (3.11) is singular of rank $(k - 1)$. On applying orthogonal transformations to the $\hat{V}_{ni}$ and $\hat{U}_{ni}$ it follows from Lemmas 3.1, and 3.2, that under (3.1) each of $\sum_i \hat{V}^2_{ni}$ and $\sum_i \hat{U}^2_{ni}$ has asymptotically a chi-square distribution with $(k - 1)$ degrees of freedom and non-centrality parameters

$$\Delta_v = \lim \sum_i \nu^2_{\alpha ni}, \qquad \Delta_u = \lim \sum_i \nu^2_{\beta ni}.$$

From (iii) of Lemma 3.2, the non-centrality parameter of $\hat{M}_n$ is $\Delta_v + \Delta_u = D_M$ say, so that

$$D_M = \lim \sum_i (\nu^2_{\alpha ni} + \nu^2_{\beta ni}). \tag{3.13}$$

Upon expanding the quantities $\nu_{\alpha ni}$ and $\nu_{\beta ni}$ and integrating by parts, it is easily seen that D_M is equal to Δ_M given in (3.12). The proof is thus complete.

4. Asymptotic efficiency. The classical test statistic Q_n for the hypothesis (1.2) is based on the difference between the least squares estimates of α_i and β_i when (1.1) is true, and the estimates of α and β when (1.2) is true. Q_n is the variance ratio criterion which in this case becomes

$$Q_n = \sum_i \{n_i(Y_{i.} - Y_{..})^2 + C^2_{ni}(\bar{\beta}_i - \bar{\bar{\beta}})^2\}/(2k - 2)s_e^2, \tag{4.1}$$

where the least squares estimates $\bar{\beta}_i$ and $\bar{\bar{\beta}}$ are given by

$$\bar{\beta}_i = C^{-2}_{ni}\{\sum_j (x_{ij} - x_{i.})(Y_{ij} - Y_{i.})\}, \qquad \bar{\bar{\beta}} = \sum_i \gamma_{ni} \bar{\beta}_i, \tag{4.2}$$

with $Y_{i.} = n^{-1} \sum_j Y_{ij}$, and s_e^2 is the mean square due to error. If F is assumed to be normal, as in the classical case, then under H_0, Q_n has the variance-ratio distribution with $(2k - 2, n - 2k)$ degrees of freedom, and the test based on Q_n is in this case most powerful.

When the assumption of normality of F is dropped, the exact distribution of Q_n is not known. Although it can be shown that for any $F(y)$ for which

$$\sigma^2(F) = \{\int y^2\, dF(y) - (\int y\, dF(y))^2\} < \infty,$$

$(2k - 2)Q_n$ under H_0 has asymptotically a chi-square distribution with $(2k - 2)$ degrees of freedom and under (3.1) has asymptotically a non-central chi-square distribution with $2k - 2$ degrees of freedom and non-centrality parameter,

$$\Delta_Q = \lim E_n\{(2k - 2)s_e^2 Q_n\}/\sigma^2(F), \tag{4.3}$$

where the expectation E_n is taken with respect to P_n-probability distribution. Straightforward computations yield

$$\Delta_Q = \sum_i \{\rho_i(\xi_i - \bar{\xi}_i)^2 + \gamma_i(\theta_i - \bar{\theta})^2\}/\sigma^2(F), \tag{4.4}$$

where $\bar{\xi}$ and $\bar{\theta}$ are defined in (3.12). By the conventional method of measuring efficiency, the asymptotic efficiency of the $\hat{M}_n$-test relative to the Q_ν-test is therefore

$$\Delta_M/\Delta_Q = \{\sigma(F) \int \phi_y'(F(y))\, dF(y)/A\}^2, \tag{4.5}$$

which is the familiar efficiency expression of rank score tests relative to the classical t-test in the two-sample problem.

If $Z_n = -2 \log L$, where L is the likelihood ratio criterion, it follows that for $F(y)$ with a finite Fisher information $I(F)$, the efficiency of the $\hat{M}_n$ test relative to the asymptotically optimum parametric Z_n-test is

$$\Delta_M/\Delta_Z = [\int \psi_y'\{F(y)\}\, dF(y)]^2/A^2I(F)\,, \tag{4.6}$$

which is unity if $A^2 = I(F)$.

Acknowledgment. I wish to thank the Associate Editor and the referee for their very useful comments on this paper.

REFERENCES

[1] Adichie, J. N. (1967). Estimates of regression based on rank tests. *Ann. Math. Statist.* **38** 894–904.

[2] Adichie, J. N. (1974). Rank score comparison of several regression parameters. *Ann. Statist.* **2** 396–402.

[3] Hájek, J. (1968). Asymptotic normality of simple linear rank statistics under alternatives. *Ann. Math. Statist.* **39** 325–346.

[4] Hájek, J. (1969). *Nonparametric Statistics.* Holden-Day, San Francisco.

[5] Sen, P. K. (1969). On a class of rank order tests for the parallelism of several regression lines. *Ann. Math. Statist.* **40** 1668–1683.

[6] Sen, P. K. (1972). On a class of aligned rank order tests for the identity of the intercepts of several regression lines. *Ann. Math. Statist.* **43** 2004–2012.

Faculty of Science
University of Nigeria
Nsukka, Nigeria

This article was written in 1975

RANK TESTS OF SUB-HYPOTHESES IN THE GENERAL LINEAR REGRESSION

BY J. N. ADICHIE

University of Nigeria, Nsukka and University of Sheffield

This paper considers the general linear regression model $Y_i = \sum_j \beta_j x_{ij} + \varepsilon_i$, and studies the problem of testing hypotheses about some of the β's while regarding others as nuisance parameters. The test criteria discussed, which are based on ranks of residuals, are shown to be asymptotically distribution-free.

0. Introduction and summary. In the general linear model $Y = X\beta + \varepsilon$, rank methods for testing hypotheses about the entire β (e.g., $\beta = 0$) have been discussed under various regularity conditions by many authors, e.g., Adichie (1967a), Koul (1969). But the methods suggested by these authors do not easily carry over to the case where there are nuisance parameters. However, Koul (1970) proposed a rank order test for $\beta_1 = 0$ in the case where $\beta' = (\beta_1, \beta_2)$ has only two components; see also Puri and Sen (1973).

In this paper we construct and study rank order statistics suitable for testing the general subhypotheses in linear regression models of full rank. Sections 1 and 2 contain the construction of a class of signed-rank and rank test statistics respectively, while in Section 3 the asymptotic distribution of the proposed classes of statistics is established. In Section 4, the asymptotic performance of the proposed test is compared with that of the classical procedure, and in Section 5, the asymptotic optimality of the test is discussed. Finally in Section 6, the general result is applied not only to the problem considered by Koul (1970) but also to the important problem of testing linearity in polynomial regression.

1. Signed-rank test statistics. Consider the general linear model

$$Y = X\beta + \varepsilon \,, \tag{1.1}$$

where Y is an $n \times 1$ vector of independent observations, X is an $n \times p$ matrix of known constants, β is a $p \times 1$ vector of unkown regression parameters such that

$$E(\varepsilon) = 0 \,; \qquad E(\varepsilon\varepsilon') = \sigma^2 I_n \,, \quad \sigma > 0 \tag{1.2}$$

where I_n is the identity matrix of order n. It is convenient to write $X = (X_1, X_2)$ so that (1.1) may be put in the form

$$Y = X_1\beta_1 + X_2\beta_2 + \varepsilon \,, \tag{1.3}$$

Received November 1975; revised August 1977.

AMS 1970 *subject classifications.* Primary 62G10; Secondary 62E20.

Key words and phrases. Asymptotic distribution, asymptotic optimality, contiguous, linear rank statistics.

where X_1 and X_2 are of order $n \times k$ and $n \times (p-k)$ respectively, while β_1 and β_2 are $k \times 1$ and $(p-k) \times 1$ subvectors of β respectively. We want to test

$$H_0: \beta_1 = 0\,, \qquad \beta_2 \text{ unspecified,} \tag{1.4}$$

against the alternative that $\beta_1 \neq 0$.

The precise functional form of the distribution function $F(y/\sigma)$ of the components of ε need not be known, but in this section we shall assume that it satisfies the following:

ASSUMPTION A. The distribution F has a symmetric density f which is absolutely continuous such that the Fisher information $I(F) = \int (f'/f)^2\, dF$ is finite, where f' denotes derivative.

In what follows, we shall be concerned with sequences of vectors of random variables $\{Y_n\}$ and nonrandom matrices $\{X_n\}$, $n = 1, 2, \cdots$, but for simplicity of notation we shall not emphasize the dependence on n. While all limits are taken as n tends to infinity, the number p of parameters remains fixed. We shall write the design matrix variously as $X = ((x_{ij})) = (x_1, \cdots, x_p)$, where x_j denotes the jth column of X. Here assume that X satisfies the Kraft and van Eeden (1972) conditions, namely:

ASSUMPTION B.

(i) $\{\max_i x_{ij}^2 / \sum_i x_{ij}^2\} \to 0$, for each $j = 1, \cdots, p$,
(ii) rank of X, $r(X) = p$,
(iii) $n^{-1}(X'X)$ tends to a positive definite matrix $\Sigma = ((\sigma'_{jj}))$,
(iv) for each pair, j, k ($j \neq k, j, k = 1, \cdots, p$) there exists a number $\gamma_{jk} \neq 0$, such that for $n > n_0$,

(a) $x_{ij}(x_{ij} + \gamma_{jk} x_{ik}) \geqq 0$ for all i
(b) $|x_j|$ and $|x_j + \gamma_{jk} x_k|$ are similarly ordered.

Two vectors u and v are similarly ordered if

$$(u_i - u_s)(v_i - v_s) \geqq 0 \qquad \text{for all} \quad i\,,\ s\,. \tag{1.5}$$

REMARK. Because of B(iv), the regression model described in this section does not cover the whole class of regression models of full rank that are usually treated by the least squares method.

Now let

$$\psi(i/(n+1)) = \psi_n(i)\,, \qquad i = 1, \cdots, n \tag{1.6}$$

be the scores generated by a function $\psi(u)$ on (0, 1), satisfying the following condition:

ASSUMPTION C. $\psi(u)$ is expressible as a difference between two monotone nonnegative square integrable functions, such that $\int \psi^2(u)\, du > 0$.

For later use, define

$$\psi(u, f) = -(f'/f)(F^{-1}((u+1)/2))\,, \qquad 0 < u < 1\,, \tag{1.7}$$

and note that $I(F)$ defined in Assumption A may also be written as

$$I(F) = \int \psi^2(u, f)\, du \,. \tag{1.8}$$

We also need an estimate $\hat{\beta}_2$ of the unspecified parameter β_2. For that introduce the notation $\|\beta\| = (\beta'\beta)^{\frac{1}{2}}$, and assume that the estimate satisfies the following two conditions:

ASSUMPTION D.

(i) The term $n^{\frac{1}{2}}\|\hat{\beta}_2 - \beta_2\|$ is $O_p(1)$ as $n \to \infty$, where p refers to probability under (1.4),

(ii) For all β_2, $\hat{\beta}_2(Y - X_2\beta_2) = \hat{\beta}_2(Y) - \beta_2$, where $\hat{\beta}_2(Y)$ denotes the estimate computed from Y.

Note that the usual least squares estimate computed under H_0 satisfies Assumption D.

Now for each $i = 1, \cdots, n$, set

$$Y_i(\hat{\beta}_2) = \hat{Y}_i = (Y - X_2\hat{\beta}_2)_i \tag{1.9}$$

where the extreme right-hand side of (1.9) denotes the ith component of the residual vector $Y - X_2\hat{\beta}_2$.

Define an n-component vector by

$$\Psi(\hat{\beta}_2) = \{\psi_n(\hat{R}_i) \operatorname{sgn} \hat{Y}_i,\ i = 1, \cdots, n\}' \tag{1.10}$$

where $\operatorname{sgn} y = 1$ or -1 according as $y > $ or < 0, and $\hat{R}_i$ is the rank of the absolute value $|\hat{Y}_i|$ among $|\hat{Y}_1|, \cdots, |\hat{Y}_n|$. For each $j = 1, \cdots, p$, set

$$s_j(\hat{\beta}_2) = \hat{s}_j = x_j'\Psi(\hat{\beta}_2)/A \tag{1.11}$$

where

$$A^2 = \int \psi^2(u)\, du \,. \tag{1.12}$$

Also write the vector of statistics in (1.11) as

$$S(\hat{\beta}_2) = \hat{S} = (\hat{s}_1, \cdots, \hat{s}_p)' = X'\Psi(\hat{\beta}_2)/A \tag{1.13}$$

and let $\hat{S}' = (\hat{S}_1', \hat{S}_2')$ be its partition such that

$$\hat{S}_2 = (\hat{s}_{k+1}, \cdots, \hat{s}_p)' = X_2'\Psi(\hat{\beta}_2)/A \,, \tag{1.14}$$

the signed-rank statistic to be considered, is

$$\begin{aligned} M(\hat{\beta}_2) = \hat{M} &= \hat{S}'(X'X)^{-1}\hat{S} - \hat{S}_2'(X_2'X_2)^{-1}\hat{S} \\ &= \Psi'(\hat{\beta})W\Psi(\hat{\beta})/A^2 \,, \end{aligned} \tag{1.15}$$

where W is a symmetric idempotent matrix of order $n \times n$ defined by

$$W = X(X'X)^{-1}X' - X_2(X_2'X_2)^{-1}X_2' \,. \tag{1.16}$$

Observe that W is orthogonal with X_2 in the sense that

$$WX_2 = 0 \,. \tag{1.17}$$

Furthermore

(1.18) $$WX_1 = \{I_n - X_2(X_2'X_2)^{-1}X_2'\}X_1 .$$

This property of orthogonality of W and X_2 which is crucial in the distribution theory of the least squares criterion, will also be very useful (see proof of Lemma 3.1 below) in the distribution theory of our rank statistics. It is primarily to achieve this orthogonality (and avoid imposing the unnecessary condition $X_1'X_2 = 0$) that motivates our use of W as the weighting function. It will be shown in Section 3 that $\hat{M}$ provides an asymptotically distribution-free statistic for testing the hypothesis (1.4). The test rejects the hypothesis if $\hat{M}$ is large. In order to consider the asymptotic power performance of $\hat{M}$, it will be necessary to find its limiting distribution not only under (1.4) but also under a sequence of Pitman alternatives:

(1.19) $$H_n: \beta_1 = n^{-\frac{1}{2}}b_1 , \quad \|b_1\| < C .$$

We now state the main theorem, the proof of which is given in Section 3.

THEOREM 1.1. *Under Assumptions* A—D

(1.20) $$\lim P_0(\hat{M} \leqq y) = P(\chi_k^2 \leqq y)$$

(1.21) $$\lim P_n(\hat{M} \leqq y) = p(\chi_k^2(\Delta_{\hat{M}}) \leqq y)$$

where $\chi_k^2(\Delta_{\hat{M}})$ *denotes the chi-square random variable with k degrees of freedom and noncentrality parameter.*

(1.22) $$\Delta_{\hat{M}} = \lim n^{-1}\{b_1'X_1'WX_1b_1\}K_F^2(\psi)$$

and

(1.23) $$K_F(\psi) = \int \psi(u)\psi(u, f)\, du/A$$

while P_0 *and* P_n *denote probabilities under* (1.4) *and* (1.19) *respectively.*

2. Rank test statistics. Rank statistics, as different from signed-rank statistics of Section 1, may also be used to construct the test statistic in the case where the design matrix X satisfies a set of assumptions specified in B_1 below. Such rank tests are briefly discussed in this section.

Consider now the model

(2.1) $$Y = X\theta + \varepsilon$$

where Y is an $n \times 1$ vector of independent observations, X is an $n \times p_1$ design matrix, θ is a $p_1 \times 1$ vector of unknown regression parameters and ε satisfies (1.2). Rewrite (2.1) as

(2.2) $$Y = X_1\theta_1 + X_2\theta_2 + \varepsilon$$

where X_1 and X_2 are of order $n \times k$ and $n \times (p_1 - k)$ respectively, while θ_1 and θ_2 are subvectors of θ. The problem is to test

(2.3) $$H_0: \theta_1 = 0 , \qquad \theta_2 \text{ unspecified}$$

against the alternative that $\theta_1 \neq 0$.

The common distribution function $F(y/\sigma)$ of the components of ε shall be in this section assumed to satisfy:

ASSUMPTION A_1. The distribution F has a density f which is absolutely continuous such that the Fisher information $I(F)$ is finite. As for the design matrix X, let

$$Z = X - \bar{X} = ((x_{ij} - \bar{x}_j)) = ((z_{ij})) ,$$

where $\bar{x}_j = n^{-1} \sum_i x_{ij}$, and let $Z = (Z_1, Z_2)$ correspond to $X = (X_1, X_2)$. We shall also write $Z = (z_1, \cdots, z_{p_1})$, and assume that X is such that Z satisfies the Kraft and van Eeden (1972) conditions, namely:

ASSUMPTION B_1.

(i) $\max_i \{z_{ij}^2 / \sum_i z_{ij}^2\} \to 0$, for each $j = 1, \cdots, p_1$;
(ii) rank of Z, $r(Z) = p_1$;
(iii) $n^{-1}(Z'Z)$ tends to a positive definite matrix $\Sigma^* = ((\sigma_{jj}^{*\prime}))$;
(iv) for each pair j, k ($j \neq k$, $j, k = 1, \cdots, p_1$), there exists a number $\gamma_{jk} \neq 0$ such that for $n > n_0$, z_j and $z_j + \gamma_{jk} z_k$ are similarly ordered.

REMARKS.

1. Because $r(X) \leq r(Z) + r(\bar{X})$ and $r(X) \leq p_1$, B_1(ii) will be satisfied only for some X in (2.1) for which $r(X) < p_1 + 1$, i.e., for some X with full rank p_1 or less. A particular class of X for which B_1(ii) holds is any orthogonal design matrix with $\bar{x}_1 = \cdots = \bar{x}_{p_1}$. Observe on the other hand that B(ii) of Section 1 holds for all X of full rank.
2. Because of B_1(ii), (iii), and (iv), the rank score method described in this section cannot be used in all linear models of full rank where the least squares method usually succeeds.
3. The testing procedure considered in this section is also valid under Jurečková (1971) conditions on X.

We shall require that the scores

$$\phi(i/(n+1)) = \phi_n(i) , \qquad i = 1, \cdots, n \tag{2.4}$$

are generated by a function $\phi(u)$ on (0, 1) that satisfies

ASSUMPTION C_1. $\phi(u)$ is nonconstant and is expressible as a difference between two montone square integrable functions on (0, 1). Put

$$A^2(\phi) = \int (\phi(u) - \bar{\phi})^2 \, du \; ; \quad \bar{\phi} = \int \phi(u) \, du . \tag{2.5}$$

As in (1.7) define for later use the function

$$\phi(u, f) = -(f'/f)(F^{-1}(u)) , \qquad 0 < u < 1 , \tag{2.6}$$

and set

$$K_F(\phi) = \int \phi(u)\phi(u, f) \, du / A(\phi) . \tag{2.7}$$

The estimate $\tilde{\theta}_2$ of the unspecified θ_2 is required to satisfy two conditions:

ASSUMPTION D_1.

(i) The term $n^{\frac{1}{2}}\|\tilde{\theta}_2 - \theta_2\|$ is $O_p(1)$ as $n \to \infty$; where p refers to probability under (2.3);

(ii) For all θ_2, $\tilde{\theta}_2(Y - Z_2\theta_2) = \tilde{\theta}_2(Y) - \theta_2$, where $\tilde{\theta}_2(Y)$ denotes the estimate computed from Y.

For each i set

$$Y_i(\tilde{\theta}_2) = \tilde{Y}_i = (Y - Z_2\tilde{\theta}_2)_i$$

and define an n-component vector by

$$\Phi(\tilde{\theta}_2) = \{\phi_n(\tilde{R}_i), i = 1, \cdots, n\}' \tag{2.8}$$

where $\tilde{R}_i$ is the rank of $\tilde{Y}_i$ in the ranking of n variables $\tilde{Y}_1, \cdots, \tilde{Y}_n$. Observe that the vector $\{\tilde{R}_i, i = 1, \cdots, n\}$ remains unchanged if instead of $\tilde{Y}_i$ we rank $(Y - X_2\tilde{\theta}_2)_i$, $i = 1, \cdots, n$. Now write

$$S(\tilde{\theta}_2) = \tilde{S} = (\tilde{s}_1, \cdots, \tilde{s}_{p_1})' = Z'\Phi(\tilde{\theta}_2)/A(\phi) \tag{2.9}$$

where

$$s_j(\tilde{\theta}_2) = \tilde{s}_j = z_j'\Phi(\tilde{\theta}_2)/A(\phi), \qquad j = 1, \cdots, p_1. \tag{2.10}$$

Form the partition $\tilde{S} = (\tilde{S}_2'\tilde{S}_2')$, and the proposed rank statistics can then be written as

$$\begin{aligned} M(\tilde{\theta}_2) = \tilde{M} &= \tilde{S}'(Z'Z)^{-1}\tilde{S} - \tilde{S}_2'(Z_2'Z_2)^{-1}\tilde{S}_2 \\ &= \Phi'(\tilde{\theta}_2)\tilde{W}\Phi(\tilde{\theta}_2)/A^2(\phi), \end{aligned} \tag{2.11}$$

where $\tilde{W}$ is the symmetric idempotent matrix of order $n \times n$ obtained from (1.16) by writing Z instead of X. In using $M(\tilde{\theta})$ for the testing problem, the hypothesis (2.3) is rejected for large values of $\tilde{M}$.

If we consider a sequence of alternatives

$$H_n: \theta_1 = n^{-\frac{1}{2}}\theta_1, \quad \|\theta_1\| < c, \tag{2.12}$$

we can state the main result of this section, which is analogous to the result of Section 1, as follows:

THEOREM 2.1. *Under the Assumptions* A_1—D_1,

$$\lim P_0(\tilde{M} \le y) = P(\chi_k^2 \le y) \tag{2.13}$$

$$\lim P_n(\tilde{M} \le y) = P(\chi_k^2(\Delta_M^*) \le y) \tag{2.14}$$

where $\chi_k^2(\Delta_M^*)$ *is the chi-square random variable with* k *degrees of freedom and noncentrality parameter*

$$\Delta_M^* = \lim n^{-1}\{\theta_1'Z_1'\tilde{W}Z_1\theta_1\}K_F^2(\phi) \tag{2.15}$$

while P_0 *and* P_n *denote probabilities under* (2.3) *and* (2.12) *respectively*.

3. Proofs of theorems. It is to be noticed that the $\hat{s}_j$'s defined in (1.11) are not the ordinary linear rank statistics because the residuals $\hat{Y}_i$ in (1.9) are not independent random variables. Now let $M(\hat{\beta}_2)$, see (1.15), be the signed-rank statistic formed from ranks of absolute values of the unobservable random variables $Y_i(\beta_2) = (Y - \chi_2\beta_2)_i$, $i = 1, \cdots, n$. We now prove

LEMMA 3.1. *If the assumptions of Theorem* 1.1 *hold then* $M(\hat{\beta}_2)$ *and* $M(\beta_2)$ *have the same limiting distribution under* H_0 *and* H_n *of* (1.4) *and* (1.19) *respectively.*

PROOF. Under H_0, $Y(\beta_2)$ is a vector of independent identically distributed random variables while $Y(\hat{\beta}_2) = Y(\beta_2) - X_2(\hat{\beta}_2 - \beta_2)$. By Assumption D(ii), we may take $\beta_2 = 0$. By D(i), there exists a number K such that $P\{\|\hat{\beta}_2\| \leq n^{-\frac{1}{2}}K\}$ is arbitrarily close to one for all $n > n_0$. It follows that for each $j = 1, \cdots, p$, the quantity

$$n^{-\frac{1}{2}}|s_j(\hat{\beta}_2) - s_j(0) + x_j'X_2\hat{\beta}_2K_F(\psi)|$$

will be with arbitrarily high probability bounded by

$$\sup_{\|b_2\| \leq n^{-\frac{1}{2}}K} |n^{-\frac{1}{2}}\{s_j(b_2) - s_j(0) + x_j'\chi_2 b_2 K_F(\psi)\}| .$$

But by Theorem 7.2 of Kraft and van Eeden (1972), as $n \to \infty$,

$$\sup_{\|b_2\| \leq n^{-\frac{1}{2}}K} \|n^{-\frac{1}{2}}\{S(b_2) - S(0) + X'X_2K_F(\psi)\}\| = o_p(1) , \tag{3.0}$$

so that under D(i) as $n \to \infty$,

$$\|n^{-\frac{1}{2}}\{S(\hat{\beta}_2) - S(0) + X'X_2\hat{\beta}_2K_F(\psi)\}\| = o_p(1) . \tag{3.1}$$

Observing that $\hat{S}(X'X)^{-1}\hat{S}$ may be written as $(n^{-\frac{1}{2}}\hat{S})'\{n(X'X)^{-1}\}(n^{-\frac{1}{2}}\hat{S})$, and that $n(X'X)^{-1} \to \Sigma$, it follows from (1.15) and (3.1) that the difference between $M(\hat{\beta}_2)$ and

$$\begin{aligned} &S'(0)(X'X)^{-1}S(0) - \hat{\beta}_2'(X_2'X)(X'X)^{-1}S(0)K_F(\psi) \\ &\quad - S'(0)(X'X)^{-1}(X'X_2)\hat{\beta}_2K_F(\psi) \\ &\quad + \hat{\beta}_2'(X_2'X)(X'X)^{-1}X'X_2\hat{\beta}_2K_F^2(\psi) - S_2'(X_2'X_2)^{-1}S_2(0) \\ &\quad + \hat{\beta}_2'S_2(0)K_F(\psi) + S_2'(0)\hat{\beta}_2K_F(\psi) - \hat{\beta}_2'X_2'X_2\hat{\beta}_2K_F^2(\psi) , \end{aligned} \tag{3.2}$$

converges to zero in probability.

Now from the identity $\{I - X(X'X)^{-1}X'\}X = 0$ we have

$$X_2 - X(X'X)^{-1}X'X_2 = 0 . \tag{3.3}$$

On writing

$$S(0) = X'\Psi(0)/A , \qquad S_2(0) = X_2'\Psi(0)/A \tag{3.4}$$

as in (1.13) and (1.14), and making repeated use of (3.3) and (3.4), the quantity in (3.2) reduces to

$$\begin{aligned} &S'(0)(X'X)^{-1}S(0) - \hat{\beta}_2'X_2'\Psi(0)K_F(\psi)/A - \Psi'(0)X_2\hat{\beta}_2K_F(\psi)/A \\ &\quad + \hat{\beta}_2'X_2'X_2\hat{\beta}_2K_F^2(\psi) - S_2'(0)(X_2'X_2)^{-1}S_2(0) \\ &\quad + \hat{\beta}_2'X_2'\Psi(0)K_F(\psi)/A + \Psi'(0)X_2\hat{\beta}_2K_F(\psi)/A - \hat{\beta}_2'X_2'X_2\hat{\beta}_2K_F^2(\psi) , \end{aligned}$$

which is easily seen to be equal to

$$S'(0)(X'X)^{-1}S(0) - S_2'(0)(X_2'X_2)^{-1}S_2(0) = M(0) .$$

That $M(\hat{\beta}_2)$ and $M(\beta_2)$ have the same limiting distribution under H_n follows from the fact that the sequence of distributions under H_n is contiguous to that under H_0. The proof of the lemma is thus complete.

For the asymptotic distribution of $M(\beta_2)$ it is convenient using well-known transformations to rewrite the matrix W, and hence $M(\beta_2)$; so put

$$(3.5) \qquad X = LB\,; \qquad X_2 = LB_2$$

where B is a $p \times p$ upper triangular matrix with positive diagonal elements, L is an $n \times p$ semi-orthogonal matrix and B_2 is a $p \times (p - k)$ matrix with

$$(3.6) \qquad (X'X) = (B'B)\,; \qquad X_2'X_2 = B_2'B_2 : L'L = I_p\,.$$

On applying this transformation, W reduces to

$$(3.7) \qquad W = L\{I_p - DD'\}L' = LVL'\,,$$

where we have written D for $B_2(B_2'B_2)^{-\frac{1}{2}}$. Because V is symmetric and idempotent, if we write the matrix

$$(3.8) \qquad L = ((l_{ij})) = (l_1, \cdots, l_p)\,,$$

and define

$$(3.9) \qquad t_j(\beta_2) = l_j'\Psi(\beta_2)/A \qquad j = 1, \cdots, p\,,$$

the statistic $M(\beta_2)$ can be written as

$$(3.10) \qquad M(\beta_2) = T'(\beta_2)VT(\beta_2)\,,$$

where

$$T'(\beta_2) = (t_1(\beta_2), \cdots, t_p(\beta_2))'\,.$$

We prove

LEMMA 3.2. *Let L be as defined in* (3.5). *If X satisfies Assumption* B(i) *and* B(iii), *then*

$$(3.11) \qquad \lim \{\max_i l_{ij}^2/\textstyle\sum_i l_{ij}^2\} = 0\,, \qquad j = 1, \cdots, p\,.$$

PROOF. First note that

$$(3.12) \qquad \textstyle\sum_i l_{ij}^2 = 1\,, \qquad j = 1, \cdots, p\,.$$

Furthermore, Assumptions B(i) and B(ii) together imply

$$(3.13) \qquad \lim \{\max_i \textstyle\sum_j x_{ij}^2/n\} = 0\,,$$

and

$$(3.14) \qquad \lim \textstyle\sum_i (x_{ij}^2/n) = \sigma_j^2\,, \qquad 0 < \sigma_j^2 < \infty, j = 1, \cdots, p\,.$$

It is also known (see, e.g., Albert (1966), page 1606), that B(iii) implies

$$(3.15) \qquad \{\lambda_{\max}(X'X)/\lambda_{\min}(X'X)\} < K\,,$$

where $\lambda_{\max}(\lambda_{\min})$ denotes maximum (minimum) characteristic root. Now from

(3.5) and (3.6), we have, using Schwarz's inequality,

$$l_{ij}^2 = (\sum_k x_{ik} b_{kj})^2 \leqq \sum_k x_{ik}^2 \sum_k b_{kj}^2 ,$$

where $B^{-1} = ((b_{ij}))$ and the summation over k is from 1 to p. Now

$$\begin{aligned}\sum_k b_{kj}^2 &\leqq \sum_k \sum_j b_{kj}^2 = \operatorname{tr}(X'X)^{-1} = \sum_k \{1/\lambda_k(X'X)\}\\ &\leqq p/\lambda_{\min}(X'X) \leqq Kp^2/\sum_k \lambda_k(X'X), \quad \text{using (3.15)}\\ &= Kp^2/\sum_i \sum_j x_{ij}^2, \quad \text{so that} \quad l_{ij}^2 \leqq Kp^2 \sum_k x_{ik}^2/\sum_i \sum_j x_{ij}^2 .\end{aligned}$$

The maximum over i of the right-hand side tends to zero because of (3.13) and (3.14). This fact together with (3.12) proves (3.11).

Proof of Theorem 1.1. In view of Lemma 3.1, we restrict attention to $M(\beta_2)$ as defined in (3.10). Due to Assumption C and (3.11), it follows in the same way as in Hájek and Šidák (1967), page 166, that under H_0, $t_j(\beta_2)$ defined in (3.9) is asymptotically $N(0, 1)$, for each j. From the way $t_j(\beta_2)$ is defined, any linear combination $\sum_j \lambda_j t_j(\beta_2)$ is again a linear rank statistic whose weights $\sum_j \lambda_j l_{ij}$ satisfy (3.11). Hence under H_0, $T(\beta_2)$ is asymptotically normally distributed with mean zero and covariance matrix I_p. As for the statistic $M(\beta_2)$ of (3.10), we may from (3.7) write

$$T'(\beta_2)T(\beta_2) = T'(\beta_2)DD'T(\beta_2) + T'(\beta_2)VT(\beta_2) , \tag{3.16}$$

where both DD' and V are idempotent matrices with rank $p-k$ and k respectively. Furthermore, it is clear from Assumption B(iii) that $DD' = (n^{-\frac{1}{2}}B_2)n(B_2'B_2)^{-1}(n^{-\frac{1}{2}}B_2')$ tends to a $p \times p$ matrix, while V by definition also tends to a limiting $p \times p$ matrix. Because $T'(\beta_2)$ is asymptotically normal, and the matrices DD' and V are idempotent, it follows from a well-known theorem on distribution of quadratic forms (see, e.g., Theorem 4.16 of Graybill (1961)), that under H_0 the quadratic form $T'(\beta_2)VT(\beta_2)$ has asymptotically a chi-square distribution with k degrees of freedom. This together with (3.10) and Lemma 3.1 proves (1.20).

To prove (1.21), note that Lemma 3.1 is valid under H_n of (1.19). It follows in the same way as in Theorem VI, 2.5 page 220 of [7] that under (1.19), $T(\beta_2)$ still has a limiting normal distribution with the same covariance matrix I_p, but with different mean vector μ given by

$$\mu = \lim n^{-\frac{1}{2}}(L'X_1 b_1)K_F(\psi) .$$

From Theorem 4.16 of [6], it follows that under (1.19) $M(\beta_2)$ has asymptotically a noncentral chi-square distribution with k degrees of freedom, and noncentrality parameter $\mu'V\mu$, which in view of (3.7) reduces to Δ_M^* given in (1.22). The proof is thus complete.

Proof of Theorem 2.1. The proof, which depends on Theorem 7.1 of [11], is omitted because it is similar to the proof of Theorem 1.1.

4. Asymptotic relative efficiency. If the model given in (1.1) and (1.2) is of full rank and if the distribution of ε is normal, the usual statistic for testing (1.4) is based on the maximum likelihood ratio

(4.1) $$Q = (n - p)D_1/kD_0\,,$$

where

(4.2) $$D_1 + D_0 = (Y - X_2\hat{\beta}_2)'(Y - X_2\hat{\beta}_2)\,,$$

and

(4.3) $$D_0 = (Y - X\hat{\beta})'(Y - X\hat{\beta}) = Y'\{I_n - X(X'X)^{-1}X'\}Y$$

with $\hat{\beta}_2$ and $\hat{\beta}$ being the least squares estimates of β under (1.4) and (1.1) respectively. In this setup, Q has the variance ratio distribution with $(k, n - p)$ degrees of freedom, and the test that rejects H_0 for large values of Q is the most powerful invariant test. When the basic assumption of normality of ε is dropped, Q loses its optimality and its exact distribution is not even known. However, for any marginal distribution F of the components of ε, for which the variance $\sigma^2 = \sigma^2(F)$ is finite, it can be shown that $|n^{-1}D_0 - \sigma^2| = o_p(1)$, as $n \to \infty$ (see, for example, Theorem 3.4 of Gleser (1966), where a stronger result is proved). Furthermore, on setting $Y(\beta_2) = Y - X_2\beta_2$, D_1 may be written as

$$\begin{aligned} D_1 &= Y'WY = Y'(\beta_2)WY(\beta_2) + \beta_2'X_2'WX_2\beta_2 \\ &= Y'(\beta_2)WY(\beta_2)\,, \quad \text{due to } (1.17)\,, \\ &= Y'(\beta)LVL'Y(\beta_2) \quad \text{by } (3.7)\,, \end{aligned}$$

where $Y'(\beta_2)L = (\sum_i l_{ij}\, Y_i(\beta_2), j = 1, \cdots, p)$. It follows from (3.11) (see, for example, Theorem 3 of Gnedenko and Kolmogorov (1954), page 103) that under H_0, $L'Y(\beta_2)/\sigma$ is asymptotically normal with mean zero and covariance matrix I_p, and under H_n, of (1.19), has asymptotic mean $n^{-\frac{1}{2}}L'X_1b_1/\sigma$. We have therefore proved the following

THEOREM 4.1. *If the components of* ε *in model* (1.1) *and* (1.2) *have common distribution function* $F(y/\sigma)$ *with* $0 < \sigma < \infty$, *then*

$$\lim P_0(kQ \leq y) = P(\chi_k^2 \leq y.)$$
$$\lim P_n(kQ \leq y) = P(\chi_k^2(\Delta_Q) \leq y)$$

where P_0, P_n, *and* $\chi_k^2(\Delta)$ *are as defined in Theorem* 2.1 *and*

(4.4) $$\Delta_Q = \lim n^{-1}\{b_1'X_1'WX_1b_1\}/\sigma^2\,.$$

Thus Q provides an asymptotically distribution-free test for the class of F for which $\sigma^2(F) < \infty$.

By the conventional method of measuring the relative asymptotic efficiency of two test statistics that have chi-square distributions with the same degree of freedom, it follows from (1.22) and (4.4) that the asymptotic efficiency of $\hat{M}$ relative to the least squares criterion is

(4.5) $$e_{\hat{M},Q} = \Delta_{\hat{M}}/\Delta_Q = \sigma^2K_F^2(\psi)\,,$$

which is the standard asymptotic efficiency of rank score tests relative to the t-test in the two-sample problem.

The results of this section hold for the rank statistic $\tilde{M}$ of (2.11), if Assumption A_1 through D_1 hold. More precisely, the asymptotic efficiency of $\tilde{M}$ relative to the least squares criterion Q computed with Z instead of X, and ϕ instead of ψ is

$$e_{\tilde{M},Q} = \sigma^2 K_F^2(\phi) . \tag{4.6}$$

5. Asymptotic optimality. If the functional form of F is known, the asymptotic performance of the $\hat{M}$-tests can be improved upon. To be specific, suppose that in addition to Assumption A of Section 1, F satisfies Assumptions I—V of Wald (1943) viz:

ASSUMPTION A*.

(i) The maximum likelihood estimates $\tilde{\beta} = (\tilde{\beta}_1, \tilde{\beta}_2)'$ exist and are uniformly consistent.

(ii) $f(y, \beta)$ is twice differentiable with respect to β and $f''(y, \beta)$ is continuous in β, where $f(y, b)$ denotes $f((y - \sum_j b_j x_j)/\sigma)$.

(iii) Let $h(y, \beta)$ denote $((f''/f) - (f'/f)^2)(y, \beta)$.

(a) For any sequences $\{\beta_{n1}\}$, $\{\beta_{n2}\}$, and δ_n such that $\lim \beta_{n1} = \lim \beta_{n2} = \beta$, and $\delta_n \to 0$, we have $\lim E_{\beta_{n1}}\{\sup h(Y, \beta)\} = \lim E_{\beta_{n1}}\{\inf h(Y, \beta)\} = I(F) < \infty$ where the sup (inf) is over β in $|\beta - \beta_{n2}| \leq \delta_n$.

(b) There exists $\varepsilon > 0$, such that $E_{\beta_1}\{\sup h(Y, \beta)\}$ and $E_{\beta_1}\{\inf h(Y, \beta)\}$ are bounded for $\|\beta_1 - \beta_2\| < \varepsilon$ and $|\delta| < \varepsilon$ where the sup (inf) is over β in $\|\beta - \beta_2\| < \delta$.

(iv) $f(y, \beta)$ is twice differentiable with respect to β under the integral sign.

(v) There exists $n > 0$, such that $E_\beta|(f'/f)(Y, \beta)|^{2+n}$ is bounded.

For testing (1.4) on the basis of n observations Y of model (1.1), Wald's test statistic ((115) of Wald (1943), page 457) becomes

$$\begin{aligned} W_n^* &= \tilde{\beta}_1'[X_1'X_1 - X_1'X_2(X_2'X_2)^{-1}X_2'X_1]\tilde{\beta}_1 I(F) \\ &= \tilde{\beta}_1'X_1'WX_1\tilde{\beta}_1 I(F) , \quad \text{in view of (1.18)} . \end{aligned} \tag{5.1}$$

The test rejects (1.4) for large values of W_n^*. To study the optimality of W_n^*, define a surface $S_c(b)$ by

$$\begin{aligned} S_c(b) = \{b\colon & b_1'[X_1'X_1 - X_1'X_2(X_2'X_2)^{-1}X_2'X_1]b_1 I(F) = c, \\ & b_2 = \beta_2 - \gamma_{22}^{-1}\gamma_{21}b_1\} \end{aligned} \tag{5.2}$$

where γ_{21}, γ_{22} are parts of a partitioned $p \times p$ nonsingular matrix

$$\gamma = \begin{pmatrix} \gamma_{11} & 0 \\ \gamma_{21} & \gamma_{22} \end{pmatrix} \tag{5.3}$$

satisfying $\gamma(X'X)\gamma' = I_p$.

Also consider the transformation $b^* = \gamma b$ where γ is as defined in (5.3). This transformation transforms the surface $S_c(b)$ into a sphere $S_c'(b)$ given by

$$b_1^{*\prime} b_1^* = C\,, \qquad b_2^* = \gamma_{21} b_2 + \gamma_{22} b_2\,.$$

Finally, for any point b_0 and any $\delta > 0$ consider the set $\omega(b_0, \delta)$ consisting of all points b which lie on the same $S_c(b)$ as b_0 and for which $|b - b_0| < \delta$. Let

$$\eta(b) = \lim_{\delta \to 0} \{A(\omega'(b, \delta))/A(\omega(b, \delta))\}\,, \tag{5.4}$$

where $\omega'(b, \delta)$ is the image of $\omega(b, \delta)$ by the transformation $b^* = \gamma b$, and $A(\omega)$ denotes the area of the set ω.

Collecting together Theorems IV, V, and VI (pages 459, 461, and 462) of Wald (1943), we have

THEOREM 5.1 (Wald). *Let* $S_c(b)$ *be the surface defined in* (5.2), *and* $\eta(b)$ *the weight function in* (5.4). *If Assumptions* A*, B(i), *and* B(ii) *hold, then for testing* (1.4), *the* W_n^**-test given in* (5.1)

(a) *has asymptotically best average power with respect to* $S_c(b)$ *and* $\eta(b)$,
(b) *has asymptotically best constant power on* $S_c(b)$,
(c) *is an asymptotically most stringent test.*

For the definitions of the asymptotic optimality in (a), (b), and (c) of the above theorem, see Definitions VIII, X, and XII at pages 453, 454, and 455 respectively of Wald (1943).

Now let $L_n = -2 \log \lambda_n$, where λ_n is the likelihood ratio statistic for testing (1.4). It is shown in Wald ((1943), page 478, (199)), that under the conditions of Theorem 5.1, and on the assumption that the L_n-test is uniformly consistent (Assumption VII, page 472 of [13]),

$$W_n^* + 2 \log \lambda_n \to 0 \quad \text{in } P_\beta\text{-probability, uniformly in} \quad \beta\,, \tag{5.5}$$

where P_β denotes probability under the assumption that β is the true parameter point.

It follows from (5.5) and Theorem 5.1 that the L_n-test has the same asymptotic optimality properties as W_n^*. Furthermore it is proved in Theorem IX, page 480 of Wald (1943), that if Assumptions A*, B(i), and B(ii) hold, and the L_n-test is uniformly consistent, then under (1.4), L_n (or W_n^*) has asymptotically a chi-square distribution with k degrees of freedom and under (1.19) has asymptotically a noncentral chi-square distribution with k degrees of freedom and noncentrality parameter

$$\begin{aligned}\Delta_L &= \lim n^{-1} b_1'[X_1'X_1 - X_1'X_2(X_2'X_2)^{-1}X_2'X_1] b_1 I(F) \\ &= \lim n^{-1} b_1' X_1 W X_1 b_1 I(F)\,.\end{aligned} \tag{5.6}$$

Now on comparing our signed-rank test statistic $\hat{M}$ with L_n, it follows from (1.22) and (5.6) that the asymptotic efficiency of $\hat{M}$ relative to L_n is

$$e_{\hat{M},L} = \Delta_{\hat{M}}/\Delta_L = K_F^2(\psi)/I(F) \tag{5.7}$$

which is unity if $K_F^2(\psi) = I(F)$, and from (1.8), (1.12), and (1.23), this equation holds if $\psi(u) = \psi(u, f)$. Thus given F that satisfies Assumptions A and A* and for which L_n is uniformly consistent, if we choose $\psi(u) = \psi(u, f)$, the method described in Section 1 will yield an asymptotically optimal test in the sense that the asymptotic efficiency of $\hat{M}_{\text{opt.}}$, the resulting signed-rank test statistic relative to (Theorem 5.1) asymptotically optimal test L_n, is

$$e_{\hat{M}_{\text{opt.}},L} = 1 . \tag{5.8}$$

A similar result holds for the rank test $\tilde{M}$ of (2.11) if Assumptions A*, A_1—D_1, and uniform consistency of L_n hold, and we take $\phi(u)$ of Assumption C_1 to be $\phi(u, f)$ defined in (2.6) and compute the L_n statistic with Z instead of X.

6. Application and example. First let us apply the method of rank statistic of Section 2 to the testing problem considered by Koul (1970), i.e., testing $\theta_1 = 0$ in the model defined in (2.1) and (1.2) with $p_1 = 2$ and $k = 1$. We then have

$$\tilde{s}_j = \textstyle\sum_i z_{ij}\phi_n(\tilde{R}_i)/A(\phi)\,, \quad z_{ij} = (x_{ij} - \bar{x}_j) \qquad j = 1, 2\,, \tag{6.1}$$

where the estimate $\tilde{\theta}_2$ used in obtaining the ranks $\tilde{R}_i$ of $Y_i(\tilde{\theta}_2)$, $i = 1, \cdots, n$, could be either the least squares estimate or the estimate considered by Puri and Sen (1973), since each of them satisfies Assumption D_1. The statistic given in (2.11) may now be written as

$$\tilde{M} = |Z'Z|^{-1}\{\tilde{s}_1^{\,2}z_2'z_2 - 2\tilde{s}_1\tilde{s}_2 z_1'z_2 + \tilde{s}_2^{\,2}z_1'z_1\} - \tilde{s}_2^{\,2}/z_2'z_2\,. \tag{6.2}$$

Observe that Koul's statistic is $n^{-1}\sum_i x_{i1}\phi_n(\tilde{R}_i)$, which is equivalent to $\tilde{s}_1$ given in (6.1). However, if $z_1'z_2 = 0$, our test can be based on $\tilde{s}_1'(z_1'z_1)^{-1}\tilde{s}_1 = \tilde{s}_1^{\,2}/z_1'z_1$, and Koul's test is a special case of this. Note also that $z_1'z_2 = 0$ is one of the sufficient conditions for Koul's test to be asymptotically distribution-free (see Lemma 2.4 of Koul (1970)).

Now, on using the transformation (3.7) as it applies to $\tilde{W}$ of (2.11), we have

$$B^* = \begin{pmatrix} b_{11} & b_{12} \\ 0 & b_{22} \end{pmatrix},$$

where

$$b_{11}^2 = z_1'z_1\,; \qquad b_{12}^2 = (z_1'z_2)^2/z_1'z_1\,; \qquad b_{22}^2 = z_2'z_2 - b_{12}^2\,. \tag{6.3}$$

With this, $\tilde{M}$ reduces to $\tilde{T}'V^{*\prime}\tilde{T}$, with $\tilde{T}' = (\tilde{t}_1, \tilde{t}_2)$ where $V^* = \{I_2 - D^*D^{*\prime}\}$, $\tilde{t}_1 = \tilde{s}_1/b_{11}$, $\tilde{t}_2 = (\tilde{s}_2/b_{22}) - (b_{12}/b_{11}b_{22})\tilde{s}_1$ and D^* is just the second column of B^*. Under the conditions of Section 2, $\tilde{M}$ has asymptotically a chi-square distribution with one degree of freedom, whether or not $z_1'z_2 = 0$. The noncentrality parameter Δ_M^* defined in (2.15) reduces in this case to

$$\lim n^{-1}\theta_1^{\,2}\{b_{11}^2 - (z_1'z_2)^2/z_2'z_2\}K_F^{\,2}(\phi)\,. \tag{6.4}$$

The test is of course consistent, since Assumption C_1 does not require symmetric $\phi(u)$ (see Theorem 2 of [12]).

Secondly, the method described in Section 1 could be used to test sub-hypotheses in polynomial regression models provided the powers of x's satisfy Assumption B. More precisely, consider the model

$$Y_i = \alpha + \beta x_i + \gamma x_i^2 + \varepsilon\,, \qquad i = 1, \cdots, n \tag{6.5}$$

which is the same as the one in (1.3) which $p = 3$, $k = 1$. Here interest is on testing H_0: $\gamma = 0$. The matrices $(X'X)^{-1}$ and $(X_2'X_2)^{-1}$ in the definition of $\hat{M}$ (1.15) are inverses of

$$(X'X) = \begin{pmatrix} n & \sum x & \sum x^2 \\ \sum x & \sum x^2 & \sum x^3 \\ \sum x^2 & \sum x^3 & \sum x^4 \end{pmatrix}$$

and $(X_2'X_2)$ which is the first principal minor of $(X'X)$.

To see what Assumption B means in this example consider a replicated design in which for each n, $x_1, \cdots, x_n$ take a fixed set of values $x_1^0, \cdots, x_c^0$ with frequencies $n_1^0, \cdots, n_c^0$. Let $\gamma_{ni}^0 = (n_i^0/n)$; then it is easy to see that Assumptions B(i), B(ii), and B(iii) are satisfied if (a) $\max_{1\le i\le c} |x_i^0| < K$; (b) for each n, $\gamma_{ni}^0 < 1$, $i = 1, \cdots, c$; (c) n_i^0 and n tend of infinity such that $\gamma_{ni}^0 \to \gamma_i^0 < 1$.

To use $\hat{M}$, we need estimates of α and β that satisfy Assumption D. These could be either the least squares estimates or the rank estimates defined in [2] computed under H_0. It is not difficult to check that the least squares estimates of α and β in the model (6.5) with $\gamma = 0$ satisfy D. That the "rank" estimates also satisfy D(ii) is a consequence of Lemma 4.1 of [2].

The three basic signed rank statistics needed for the definition of $\hat{M}$ are:

$$s_j(\hat{\alpha}, \hat{\beta}) = \hat{s}_j = \textstyle\sum_i x_i^{j-1}\psi_n(\hat{R}_i)\ \mathrm{sgn}\ \hat{Y}_i/A\,, \qquad j = 1, 2, 3\,.$$

Acknowledgment. I would like to thank the referee whose liberal comments led to a substantial improvement. I am also grateful to Professor I. Richard Savage for his many valuable suggestions.

REFERENCES

[1] Adichie, J. N. (1967a). Asymptotic efficiency of a class of nonparametric tests for regression parameters. *Ann. Math. Statist.* **38** 884–893.

[2] Adichie, J. N. (1967b). Estimates of regression parameters based on rank tests. *Ann. Math. Statist.* **38** 894–904.

[3] Albert, A. (1966). Fixed size confidence ellipsoids for linear regression parameters. *Ann. Math. Statist.* **37** 1602–1630.

[4] Gleser, L. J. (1966). Correction to "On the asymptotic theory of fixed-size sequential confidence bounds for linear regression parameters." *Ann. Math. Statist.* **37** 1053–1055.

[5] Gnedenko, B. V. and Kolmogorov, A. N. (1954). *Limit Distributions for Sums of Independent Random Variables.* Addison-Wesley, Cambridge.

[6] Graybill, F. (1961). *An Introduction to Linear Statistical Models*, **1**. McGraw-Hill.

[7] Hájek, J. and Šidák, Z. (1967). *Theory of Rank Tests.* Academic Press, New York.

[8] Jurečková, J. (1971). Nonparametric estimate of of regression coefficients. *Ann. Math. Statist.* **42** 1328–1338.

[9] Koul, H. L. (1969). Asymptotic behavior of Wilcoxon type confidence regions in multiple linear regression. *Ann. Math. Statist.* **40** 1950–1979.

[10] KOUL, H. L. (1970). A class of ADF tests for subhypotheses in the multiple linear regression. *Ann. Math. Statist.* **41** 1273–1281.

[11] KRAFT, C. H. and VAN EEDEN, C. (1972). Linearised rank estimates and signed-rank estimates for the general linear hypothesis. *Ann. Math. Statist* **43** 42–57.

[12] PURI, M. L. and SEN, P. K. (1973). A note on asymptotic distribution-free tests for subhypotheses in multiple linear regression. *Ann. Statist.* **1** 553–556.

[13] WALD, A. (1943). Tests of statistical hypotheses concerning several parameters when the number of observations is large. *Trans. Amer. Math. Soc.* **54** 426–482.

DEPARTMENT OF STATISTICS
UNIVERSITY OF NIGERIA
NSUKKA CAMPUS, NIGERIA

This article was written in 1978

CHAPTER SIX: PROFESSOR JAMES N. ADICHIE'S CURRICULUM VITAE

PERSONAL PARTICULARS:

1) Name: James Nwoye Adichie
2) Date of Birth: 1st March, 1932
3) Place of Birth: Abba, Njikoka Local Government Area, Anambra State
4) Nationality: Nigerian
5) Marital Status: Married with six children
6) Occupation/Rank: Professor of Statistics, University of Nigeria since 1st October, 1976.

UNIVERSITY EDUCATION:

1. University College, Ibadan, 1957 – 1960

B.A. Mathematics (London) 1960

2. University of California, Berkeley, 1963 – 1966

Ph.D. Statistics (California) 1966

EMPLOYMENT:

1. Lecturer, Nigerian College of Science &Technology, Enugu-Dec. 1960 – August 1961
2. Assistant Lecturer, University of Nigeria, Nsukka- Sept. 1961 – Sept. 1963
3. Staff on Study Leave at University of California, Berkeley Oct. 1963 – June 1966
4. Lecturer, University of Nigeria, Nsukka- June 1966 – June 1974
5. Senior Lecturer, University of Nigeria, Nsukka- July 1972 – June 1974

6. Reader, University of Nigeria, Nsukka, July 1974 – Sept. 1976
7. Professor, University of Nigeria Nsukka-Oct. 1976 – to Sept. 1999
8. Professor Coordinator, Statistic programme, National Mathematical Centre, Abuja Oct 1999 – Feb. 2002

ADMINISTRATIVE EXPERIENCE: IN THE UNIVERSITY OF NIGERIA

1. Headship of Department:

Acting Head of Department of Mathematics and Statistics – 1970 – 1971

- Helped to establish a separate Department of Statistics in 1973
- Head of Department of Statistics – 1973 – 1979, 1985 – 1989

2. Deanship of Faculty:

Served as Dean, Faculty of Physical Sciences: 1979/80

3. Deputy Vice-Chancellorship: Served as Deputy Vice-Chancellor, Nsukka Campus for four years – 1 August 1980 – 31 July 1984.

4. Member of Senate:

- As elected member representing Faculty of Science: 1966/67
- As Acting Head of Department of Mathematics and Statistics 1970/71
- As Head of Department of Statistics: 1973-75
- As professorial Member: 1976 – to date

5. Member of the Governing Council and Its Committees:

- Elected First of the three Senate Representatives in the Governing council in 1980, and I served in that capacity until the Council was dissolved in January 1984.
- Member of Appointments and Promotions Committee for Academic Staff: 1980 – 1984
- Member of Appointments and Promotions Committee for Senior Administrative and Technical Staff: 1980 – 1984
- Member, Finance and General Purposes Committee: 1980 – 1984
- Member, Tenders Board: 1982 – 1984
- Member, Works and Site Committee: 1980 – 1984.

Chairmanship of University Committees and Boards: Gained considerable experience in University Affairs through service on several University Committees and Boards (1961 – 1984). A short list is as follows:

a. Member, University Appraisals/Assessment Committee for Academic Staff: 1973 – 1984
b. Member, University Appraisals/Assessment Committee for Senior Technical Staff: 1973 – 79
c. Member, Committee of Deans: 1979 -1984.
d. Member, Development Committee of Senate: 1976 – 1984
e. Chairman, University Appraisals/Assessment Committee for Senior Administrative and Technical Staff: 1980 – 1984.
f. Chairman and Managing Director, University of Nigeria Bookshop Limited – 1980 – 1984.
g. Chairman, University Careers Board: 1980 – 84

h. Chairman, Action Committee on Endowment Fund: 1980 – 1984

i. Chairman, Administrative Planning Sub-Committee of the Development Committee: 1980 – 1984

ACADEMIC ACTIVITIES

i. External Examiner in Mathematics and Statistics to Ahmadu Bello University, Universities of Benin, Calabar, Ibadan, Ife and Lagos, from 1972 – 1984
ii. Visiting Fellow, University of Sheffield: 1975/76
iii. Associate Editor, Abacus, (Journal of Mathematical Association of Nigeria)
iv. First Editor, Journal of Statistical Association of Nigeria
v. Associate Editor, Journal of Nigerian Maths Society from 1980 to date.
vi. Visiting Professor, San Diego State University, California, 1984/85
vii. Reviewer For: Math. Reviews, An. Math. Statist., Ann. Statist.(American) National Science Foundation, Journal of American Statistical Association and Journ. Roy. Statist Assoc.

RESEARCH ACTIVITIES:

I. Supervised the first postgraduate student to obtain a Master's degree of the University of Nigeria in 1971 (Chief Christian Onuoha).
II. Main area of research interest is in non-parametric Methods of Statistical Analysis. It seeks to develop

new methods of analysis which are valid under realistic assumptions. I gave invited lectures on my work in Non-parametric Statistics at the following leading British Universities during the 1975/76 session: Aberystwyth, Birmingham, Sheffield, London (Imperial College), Glasgow and Cambridge.

MEMBERSHIP OF LEARNED SOCIETIES/ PROFESSIONAL ORGANIZATIONS:

Member, Institute of Mathematical Statistics
Member, Mathematical Association of Nigeria; was the General Secretary – Sept. 1971 – August 1973
Member, Science Association of Nigeria
Member, International Statistics Institute (First Nigerian full member)

MEMBERSHIP OF (NIGERIAN) NATIONAL BODY:

Member, National Advisory Council on Statistics – 1977 – 1980
Chairman, for Reorganization of Fed

RESEARCH PUBLICATIONS:

1. Adichie, J.N. (1967) -Asymptotic Efficiency of Class of non-parametric tests for regression parameters: Ann. Math. Statist.38 884 – 893.
2. Adichie, J.N. (1967) -Estimates of Regression based on rank tests: Ann. Math. Statist.38 894 – 904
3. Adichie, J.N. (1974) -Rank acore comparison of several regression parameters: Ann. Statist. 2 396 – 402.

4. Adichie, J.N. (1974) -On Some robust properties of estimates of regression based on rank tests: Ann. Statist. Math.26 (2). 223 – 231
5. Adichie, J.N. (1974) - Rank score tests for linearity of Regression of repeated observations: Communications in Statistics.3 (7)
6. Adichie, J.N. (1975) -On the use of ranks for testing the coincidence of several regression lines:Ann. Satist. 3. 521 – 7.
7. Adichie, J.N. (1975) -Non parametric C-sample tests with regression: Ann. Statist. Math.27 (2) 299 – 307.
8. Adichie, J.N. (1975) -Ranking in analysis of covariance tests: Communications in Statistics 4 (9) 883 – 890.
9. Adichie, J.N. (1976) -A note on asymptotic linearity of a rank statistics in regression parameters: Communication in Statistics. 5 (2) 171– 181.
10. Adichie, J.N. (1976) -Testing parallelism of regression lines against ordered alternatives. Communication in Statistics A 5 (ii) 985 – 997.
11. Adichie, J.N. (1978) -Rank tests of subhypothesisin the general linear regression. Ann. Statist. 6 1012 – 1026.
12. Adichie, J.N. &Afonja Biyi (1982) Statistical Education and training in the Developing Countries of Africa: Proc. First Intl. Conf. on Teaching Statistics Univ. of Shelffield, Vol. II439 – 449
13. Adichie, J.N. (1984) -Rank tests in Linear Models in Krishnaiah and Sen (eds) Handbook of Statistics 4 229 – 257. North Holland

14. Adichie, J.N. (1986) -Statistical Education in the developing countries of Africa: The Nigerian Experience: Proc. 2nd Intl. Conf. on Teaching Statist. Univ. Of Victoria,29– 32.
15. Adichie, J.N. (1988) - Training Teachers of Statistics in the developing countries of Africa: the Nigerian Experience. Proc. of Intl. Statist.Inst. Round Table Conf. Budapest (Anne Hawkins (ed) ISI 195 – 203
16. Adichie, J.N. (1989) -The development of School Statistics programme in Nigeria: Proc. 47th Session of Intl. Statist. Inst. Paris Vol I - III, Bk 2, 209 – 216.

CHAPTER SEVEN: TRIBUTES TO PROFESSOR JAMES NWOYE ADICHIE

7.1: From Wife, Mrs. Grace Adichie:

A TRIBUTE TO MY DEAR HUSBAND, PROFESSOR JAMES NWOYE ADICHIE: ODELUORA N'ABBA

J., as I have fondly called him in these fifty years plus of our lives, is a man who strongly believes that with God everything is possible. When children came, I joined them in calling him Daddy and he has been a steadfast Daddy to all of us, come rain, come shine.

This very intelligent man believes in hard work and encourages us to work hard. According to him, honest hard work is the essence of success. Anyone who has had anything to do with him will testify to his honesty. He is a man of integrity. He believes in the golden rule and abides by it. He is very loving, caring, kind, unassuming and contended with whatever he has. Our children and I adore him and pray God to give him many more happy returns and healthy years to live.

Your Wife,
Ifeoma Grace Adichie

7.2: From first daughter, Ijeoma

My Daddy-Prof J N Adichie

"Uwam, uwa ozo ngi ga bu Nnam" best translated as "In this life, and in my next life you will be my father"

I am fortunate to be blessed with a loving father, who is analytical, authentic and devoted.

He is my biggest source of strength, my all powerful dad,-whenever I call him, with any concerns in my life that involved others, he will always tell me 1- "Never Mind"; 2-He is "stronger" than their own dad- {boxing or wrestling match??} Hearing these from him, always and will continue to be my source of strength.

My Daddy is the most knowledgeable man in my life- I often asked, when I was younger, if any so called "big men" knew my dad, to me that was a measure of who was important or not. He still mentions this sometimes, when we are together and going down memory lane.

Dad is a truly affectionate man-The love he has for 6 of us and our mom-He will always say that he is a very "rich" man because he has us!

He instilled in us all, the value of education, telling us, "excel in whatever field of study you choose, and nobody can take that from you"

A deeply religious man, who has taught us all, the importance of faith and God's will for one's life. He will always say "munachimdinma" which best describes his close/personal relationship with God.

Congratulations Dad and may the good Lord continue to bless you!

Like Ari and Toks will say, you are the "BESTEST'"

Tons of Love,
Ijeoma Maduka,MD

7.3: From Second Daughter, Uchenna

TRIBUTE TO THE WORLD'S GREATEST DAD

My dad turned eighty on March 1st 2012. He is now eighty- one and a bit. This is such a big deal. It is truly a milestone and one that makes me pensive.

Dad, this is to express gratitude for the life you have given me that has led to the life I have now. I am a strong, confident and self-assured woman today because of you. Thank you, Dad.

I remember with nostalgia, when we were growing up. How you would drive us to and from school even though school was just a stone throw away. Some other parents would have their children walk to school. You always wanted to be around us, fully protecting and shielding us. Thank you. Dad.

I remember those chilly harmattan nights in Nsukka, when you would tell us folklores and tales usually about the ever sly tortoise. Those times when you would gently drum on our backs one after the other while we sang "Nne gi jelu ebe e e ?" The bond, the joy, the happiness, the peace and the togetherness you brought to us have remained with us.

I remember how you waited for me patiently under a tree on a hot sunny afternoon while I wrote my JAMB exams. That gave me a lot of inspiration and I was determined to put in my best. Little wonder then that my result was one of the best in my department. It's all thanks to you, Dad.

I remember a long time ago on a family vacation in San- Diego when I chose to buy very dark sun glasses because I thought they were cool though I wasn't quite sure whether you 'd approve of them. This made me a little uptight. You looked at me with a smile and said "As long as you can see through them, you can have them."I was so excited that I even wore them inside the house!

I can say without hesitation that I have been deeply blessed by God, privileged to call the finest man I have ever known "Dad". He is a man of immense integrity. I learnt what integrity was by watching my father live. He is a man of his words.

Daddy is a man not merely with a good mind, but one who is filled with wisdom. My siblings and I have benefitted from his sage words, delivered humbly from a heart of love and genuine concern. He is a truth teller. His mind has always been keen and analytical. He is an example of love, particularly in the way I've seen him interact with my mum. They've been married for 50 years. How Golden! He models love in how he speaks and lives.

One thing that ties all these together is that my dad is deeply committed to Jesus. He has priorities in life, and they begin with God. Thank you for inspiring us with your faith, humility, kindness and ethics.

I feel lucky and blessed to have you as my father-odelora Abba, Nigeria's first professor of Statistics. What a feat! I am mighty proud of you dad and this is why I fondly call you " E nna e e" to which you answer "E e e e", because you are just what the word means, "My father".

Thank you Dad for working so hard all those years to give us a good life.

Thank you for being a wonderful grandpa to my children, Chisom and Amaka. They really adore you. The only grandpa who can solve Further Math problems over the phone. What more could they ask for. You remain a source of inspiration and a role model to my husband, Sunny.

Thank you for always caring and staying involved. Thank you for giving me that trait of always following the rules and keeping to time- this is one of your strong points.

Thank you for being an example of helping others in the years that you've had more time on your hands after retirement.

These words have done little justice to the rich legacy of a great man, but on this milestone birthday and as you receive your well-deserved award, I feel my friends ought to know just a little about this treasure of a man many of them will never meet- but whom they meet every time they interact with me, for a little of my Dad will always, I pray shine through me.

Please lets raise a glass and toast to a perfect gentleman, my father and hero, Nigeria's first professor of Statistics, Professor James Nwoye Adichie for an award and honour well deserved, and for being what he is, a good man.

"Who the cap fits, let them wear it". Congratulations.

So Dad, stay healthy and let's enjoy many more years to come.

With all my love,
Uchy

7.4: From First Son, Chuks

My Dad at 81

I have always believed that life is the sum of your choices, but there are a few choices that one cannot make for oneself. An example is the choice of a father

I was born in 1968 and my father was 36 years old then. I can say without any hesitation or iota of doubt that I have been deeply blessed by God and that I am privileged to call the finest man I have ever known "Dad". It is with no fear of contradiction that I say that whatever I am or may yet become, by way of a worthwhile human being, I owe first and foremost to my parents, and to my Dad first as the leader of our family and example of what it means to be a man.

I could say a lot of things in tribute to my father but I lack the ability to do justice in a short piece to all that my father means to me.

My father, daddy the man, the man: is a self-sacrificing man, who is authentic in all of his dealings with others and it's because of his example, that I carefully consider the choices I make as a father; knowing I can dramatically affect the lives of my children through my choices and characteristics.

My dad is a man of great wisdom, and a very intelligent man. I have benefitted time and again from his sage words, delivered humbly from a heart of love and genuine concern. He will never force his thoughts on me, but gently guides with wisdom when he considers something important.

My dad has always been an example of love; particularly in the way I've seen him interact with my mother. They've been married 50 years now, and have given me a template of which I have based my married life on.

Growing up and today, I have so many wonderful memories of my father, which will need a book to list. I loved all the stories he used to tell us about "the olden days" which he usually starts by saying 'na oge gboo". Also, the "akuko iro" he used to tell us are still etched in my memory and sometimes do seem to come to life.

I look back now and remember a scene in my early teens when my dad swept me up and carrying up in the air out of joy when he found out I had one of the best JAMB scores. "Chu the boy" he screamed out of joy.

You see, education is top priority always for my father, as is evident from his career and renowned achievements in his chosen field as well as the well deserved title bestowed upon him – Odeluora of Abba. He taught my brothers, sister and I, to always be the best we can be and to pursue our dreams. He instills positive family values and lives by their example

This must have been passed down the generations as he still fondly tells us the stories of the sacrifices his father – David Adichie, made "na oge gboo" to ensure he got a good education. I too, have taken the baton as I continue to emulate my dad.

My dad is a devout catholic and a man of faith who completely depends on God and would never miss Sunday Mass, and did not matter which country he was in. He has taught us to handle life challenges and obstacles that come our way with faith. I've never once doubted that my dad was in our corner and would do anything he humanly could for my good, my sister's good, my brothers and my mother's good.

My dad is a template on which I try to live my life as a husband, a father and indeed a brother and continues to be a wonderful role model as a loving, caring father.

These words have done little justice to the rich legacy of a great man, but on this milestone, I felt that the world ought to know just a little about this treasure of a man whom they meet every time they interact with me, for a little bit of my dad will always, I pray, shine through me.

Daddy, I love you more than any written or spoken word can convey

Congratulations!

Chukwu gozie gi

From Chukwunwike Adichie (Chu the man)June 2003

7.5: From Second Son, Okey Adichie

TRIBUTE TO PROF J.N. ADICHIE ON HIS 81ST BIRTHDAY

Odelorankembunambuna Abba nine, It is quite amazing that you have turned 81 years: Four score and one, to borrow your mathematical term. Yet you do not look it.

You are such a selfless man with a large heart. You stand for the truth at all times. I sometimes wonder how you can keep calm in certain situations. I believe that makes you the person that you are.

It is always a pleasure to hear you tell stories of your childhood and stories of characters in the village. I remember many years ago when I was sick; you came downstairs and offered to give me a bath. I was quite able to do it myself, but you insisted. I have never been cleaner after that bath. You scrubbed me so hard with sponge and very little soap. I was quite glad when the bath was over.

Such is your heart. I thank you for being the best dad anyone could ever wish for.

May the Lord continue to bless you with good health and peace of mind. Congratulations!

From Okey Adichie

7.5: From Third Daughter, Chimamanda Ngozi Adichie

Daddy,

I knew, as a child, that my father was brilliant. I remember how you would stay up in your study until very late, reading and writing and solving statistics problems. I have always been proud of your intelligence. When I was in secondary school, you demystified mathematics for me. You encouraged me, made me believe that the problems were not as difficult as I thought. I have always been proud of what a good teacher you are. You spent hours carefully correcting your students' assignments. You gave much to your students and expected much from them. I have always been proud of how well your students speak of you, how they speak often of your integrity, your conscientiousness, your generosity of spirit. And they were right, because you exhibited those qualities at home. This is what I am proudest of: what a wonderful father you are. You are thoughtful, kind, truthful, considerate and gentle. Your calming voice has been my anchor in many troubled times. Your wisdom has adorned my life like a jewel. You are my life's greatest inspiration. Congratulations as you receive this honour. It is more than well-deserved. May God keep you healthy and happy.

Your daughter,
Chimamanda Ngozi Adichie

7.6: From Third Son, Kenechukwu Adichie

Dear Daddy,

I am fortunate to have been under your guidance when I was much younger. You instilled qualities like hard work, honesty and pride in me and these have helped me through the sometimes rocky journey to become the person I am today.

I remember when I was in secondary school, I used to ask for your help to solve certain math problems. You would rub your index finger and your thumb together while explaining it, and within minutes, a math theory that I never thought I would understand became very comprehensible. Those memories have stuck with me, and when I tutored my nephew, your grandson Toks, I tried rubbing my index finger and thumb to recreate the same experiences I had with you. We eventually got to the solution but it wasn't within minutes. Incidents like that, however trivial it may have been, made me aware of your brilliance and I was and will always be in awe of you.

"The man" (like I fondly call you) congratulations on such an honor as having your colleagues recognize your achievements in the field of academia.

From your son,
Kene Adichie

7.7: From the Head of Department of Statistics, University of Nigeria, Nsukka

A Tribute to an Erudite Professor, Professor James Nwoye Adichie: Nigeria's first Professor of Statistics

Prof James Nwoye Adichie, the first professor of Statistics in Nigeria, was born on March 1, 1932 in Abba, Njikoka Local Government Area of Anambra State.

After passing the Advanced Level General Certificate of Education ('A' level GCE) examinations in Pure mathematics, Applied mathematics, English and Latin, he was admitted into the University College Ibadan (UCI) now the University of Ibadan (UI) in 1957 to read mathematics. In those days when the UCI was a college of the University of London and was the only university institution in Nigeria, it was a remarkable achievement for a student to be admitted into the College. He graduated B.A. Mathematics of the University of London in 1960 among the top three students in a class of 13. At that time a student was awarded the B.A. degree if his/her A-Level subject combination included arts subjects in addition to the mathematics subject; and the B.Sc degree if his/her subjects combination consisted of mathematics and science subjects.

Soon after graduating, he went on to lecture first at the Nigerian College of Science and Technology, Enugu, and later at the University of Nigeria, Nsukka (UNN) until September 1963, when he proceeded to the prestigious University of California at Berkeley, USA. This is one of the greatest centres of statistical excellence in the USA, if not in the world.

Prof Adichie usually shares with his students his experience in Berkeley, this is reported inter alia "The road to Statistics from the first degree in Mathematics was r-o-u-g-h. When I got to Berkeley, I was in a class. We call it post-graduate, they call it graduate class. In that class were Chinese, Japanese, Israelis, Americans, South Americans, but most of these people have done M.A. Statistics or M.A. Mathematics in their respective Universities in their countries before coming to Berkeley, one of the best, if not the best university in Statistics in the whole of United States.

They were coming to do their PhD there. So, I was with them. Then lectures started, I didn't

understand anything. First, I was British-trained. I had the British orientation of taking exams. I went to a professor and said that I know that I had just come but I want to go. I am not finding things easy here. The man just laughed and took me to his office and told me what to do to be able to fit into the system.

In spite of the initial problem he encountered he obtained his PhD degree Statistics in a record time of three years in 1966, the first Nigerian to do so. He promptly returned to the University of Nigeria, Nsukka to start his academic carrier. On coming back to University of Nigeria, Nsukka he rose from the rank of lecturer II to full professor within a ten year period.

He held various administrative posts in University of Nigeria, Nsukka. He was the acting head of the Department of Mathematics and Statistics from 1970 to 1971. He helped to establish a separate Department of Statistics in 1973. This is the first autonomous and independent Department of statistics in the Nigerian University system. He was the first Head of this new Department from 1973 to 1979. He was also the Head of Department of statistics again in 1985 to 1989. He was the Dean of the Faculty of Physical Sciences in 1979/1980 academic session. He then served as Deputy Vice-Chancellor, University of Nigeria, Nsukka Campus for a period of four years from August 1 1980 to July 31, 1984.

He served in many University Committees in the University of Nigeria. He also served as external examiner in many first generation universities in Nigeria.

He served as associate editor in some reputable journals globally. He belongs to many local and international learned societies and professional organizations. Prof. Adichie's main area of research is Non-Parametric Methods of Statistical Analysis. These methods seek to develop new methods of analysis that are valid under realistic assumptions. He was such a renowned scholar in this field that he was invited by some leading British universities to deliver a series of lectures on his work. The universities are Cambridge, London (Imperial College), Aberystwyth, Birmingham, Sheffield, and Glasgow. At different points in his brilliant academic career, he was a visiting fellow at the University of Sheffield, England and a visiting professor at the San Diego State University, California, U.S.A.

Apart from delivering many brilliant academic papers at several workshops, conferences and seminars locally and abroad, Prof. Adichie has published numerous scholarly papers in reputable learned journals and has served as a reviewer for some of them including the Journal of the American Statistical Association, the Annals of Mathematical Statistics, the Journal of the Royal Statistical Society, Series A, etc. This erudite professor published his research findings in many top journals In statistics all over the globe,

He is a member of many learned societies including the International Statistical Institute (ISI) of which he was the first Nigerian to be elected a full ordinary member in 1978; the Institute of Mathematical Statistics, the Mathematical Association of Nigeria of which he was once the general secretary, to mention a few. Incidentally, the ISI with headquarters in The Hague, Netherlands, is the world apex statistical organization. He was the first editor of the Journal of the Statistical Association of Nigeria and at one time an associate editor of the ABACUS - Journal of the Mathematical Association of Nigeria.

At the University of Nigeria where he was a distinguished teacher of statistics for 33 years, he was the supervisor of the first post-graduate student to obtain a master's degree of the UNN in 1971/1972;

As an elected member of Council of the University, he made tremendous contributions to the progress of the university through his activities in the various committees of the Council and some other non-Council Committees. His activities are not limited to the UNN. Apart from his contribution to the development of statistics in the Nigerian university system, he played a key role in the development of the National Mathematical Centre (NMC). He, with three others, prepared for the Federal Government in 1987/88, a proposal for setting up the NMC. He later served as member of a Representative Group of Mathematical Scientists that met the Technical Expert Committee Visitation Panel for the upgrading of the NMC to the status of an International Centre for Excellence. He served the Centre in various capacities. He was a member of its academic board, a member of two of its strategic committees, and professor and coordinator of its statistics programme.. He organized the Centre's first Foundation

Post-Graduate Course on mathematical statistics and the first Foundation Post-Graduate Course on Exact and Asymptotic Statistical Inference.

The Department of Statistics is proud to be associated with the celebration of a life achievement of this intellectual giant and her first Head of department.

From

Chukwu W.I.E- Associate Professor of Statistics/Operations Research (Head of Department of Statistics, UNN as at 2013)

REFERENCES

Adichie, J.N. (2013a). *"Roots to Career". First Interview Session granted to Alex Animalu and Jeff Unaegbu,* January, at Animalu's residence in Nsukka.

Adichie, J.N. (2013b). *"My Nigerian Civil War Experience". Second Interview Session granted to Alex Animalu and Jeff Unaegbu,* June 15, at Animalu's residence in Nsukka.

Adichie, J.N. (2013c). *"My Administrative Achievements". An Interview Session granted to Jeff Unaegbu,* June 19, at Adichie's residence in Nsukka.

Adichie, J.N. (2013d). *"Career Progression and Post-Graduate Education". An Interview Session granted to Prof. Peter I. Uche,* June, at Adichie's residence in Nsukka.

Adichie, J.N. (2012). "How I Grew Up", unpublished long-hand manuscript.

Aneke, L.N. (2007). *The Untold Story of the Nigeria-Biafra War.* New York: Triumph Publishing.

Crowder, M. (1978). *The Story of Nigeria.* London: Faber & Faber.

Crowther, S. and Taylor, JC. (1859). *The Gospel on the Banks of the Niger.* London. Frank Cass Printing Press, 1968.

Ike, V.C. (1986). "The University and the Nigerian Crisis: 1966-1970" in Obiechina, E. *et al* (eds) *University of Nigeria 1960-85: An Experiment in*

Higher Education. Nsukka: University of Nigeria Press.

Kenneth Onwuka Dike (1957). *Origins of the Niger Mission.* Lagos.

Nwabara, S.N. (1977). *Iboland: A Century of Contact with Britain, 1860-1960.* London: Hodder and Stoughton.

ABOUT THE AUTHORS

Professor Alexander O.E. Animalu, Bsc. (London), MA (Cantab.) and PhD (Ibadan), FAS, NNOM, IOM, born in August 28, 1938 at Oba in Idemmili-South, Anambra State, is presently Emeritus Professor of Physics in the University of Nigeria, Nsukka. A former Director/ Chief Executive of the National Mathematical Center, Abuja, and President of the Nigerian Academy of Science, he has travelled widely as an international scholar, published interdisciplinary books, not only in the Sciences but also in the humanities. The current biography of Prof. James Nwoye Adichie is amongst the latest of the series of his well-researched biographies of eminent personalities among whom are Emeritus Prof. James O.C. Ezeilo, HRH Eze (Prof.) Ikpendu Christopher Ononogbu, Rt. Hon. (Dr.) Nnamdi Azikiwe, Prof. C.A. Onwumechili and Prof. Chike Obi. He is a recipient of the prestigious Nigerian National Order of Merit Award for Basic Sciences and Knight of St. Christopher.

Prof. Peter Ikechukwu Uche, BSc (Nigeria), MSc (Sheffield), PhD (Sheffield), FRSS, FNSA, MIS, KSM, is a Professor of Statistics. He hails from Oraukwu in Idemili North LGA of Anambra State. He came in contact with Prof. J. N. Adichie in 1966 when, as a result of the Nigerian crisis, he transferred from the University of Ibadan to the University of Nigeria, Nsukka. He graduated in 1971 with a B.Sc (First Class Hons) in Statistics, emerging as the best graduating student of the University. He later went to University of Sheffield in the United Kingdom where he obtained M.Sc and Ph.D degrees in 1973 and 1975 respectively. He is a Fellow of Nigerian Statistical Association and a Fellow of the Royal Statistical Society. As a Professor of Statistics in the University, he has been contributing to national development through the training of generations of students at all levels and to the intellectual community through his research in the area of stochastic processes.

Jeff Unaegbu (born October 1, 1979) is a Senior Cinematographer in the Institute of African Studies, University of Nigeria, Nsukka. He has authored four books of poetry, short stories, origins and history; co-authored five books of biographies, philosophy, history and psychology; co-edited two books of administration and biographical listings; and produced twenty video documentaries, including Zik of Africa: A Historical Reflection and Chinua Achebe and the Sands of Time. His 512-paged first-ever 44-year history of the Students' Union Government of the University of Nigeria, Nsukka, was second runner-up in the NUC-organized NURESDEF Arts/ Humanities (Research category) in year 2008. His Ode on Lagos, adjudged the longest published poem by a Nigerian in a Newswatch magazine book review of April 2007, was second runner-up in the ANA/ Cadbury $2000 Prize (year 2011) and first runner-up in the NUC-organized NURESDEF Arts/ Humanities (Research category) in year 2012. His full bio-data can be accessed on the Wikipedia Online Encyclopaedia.

Printed in Great Britain
by Amazon

60281358R00098